It Gets Better

And other things grieving Moms really wish you'd STOP saying

by J. Daniels

Cover design and chapter illustration by Annalily Daniels

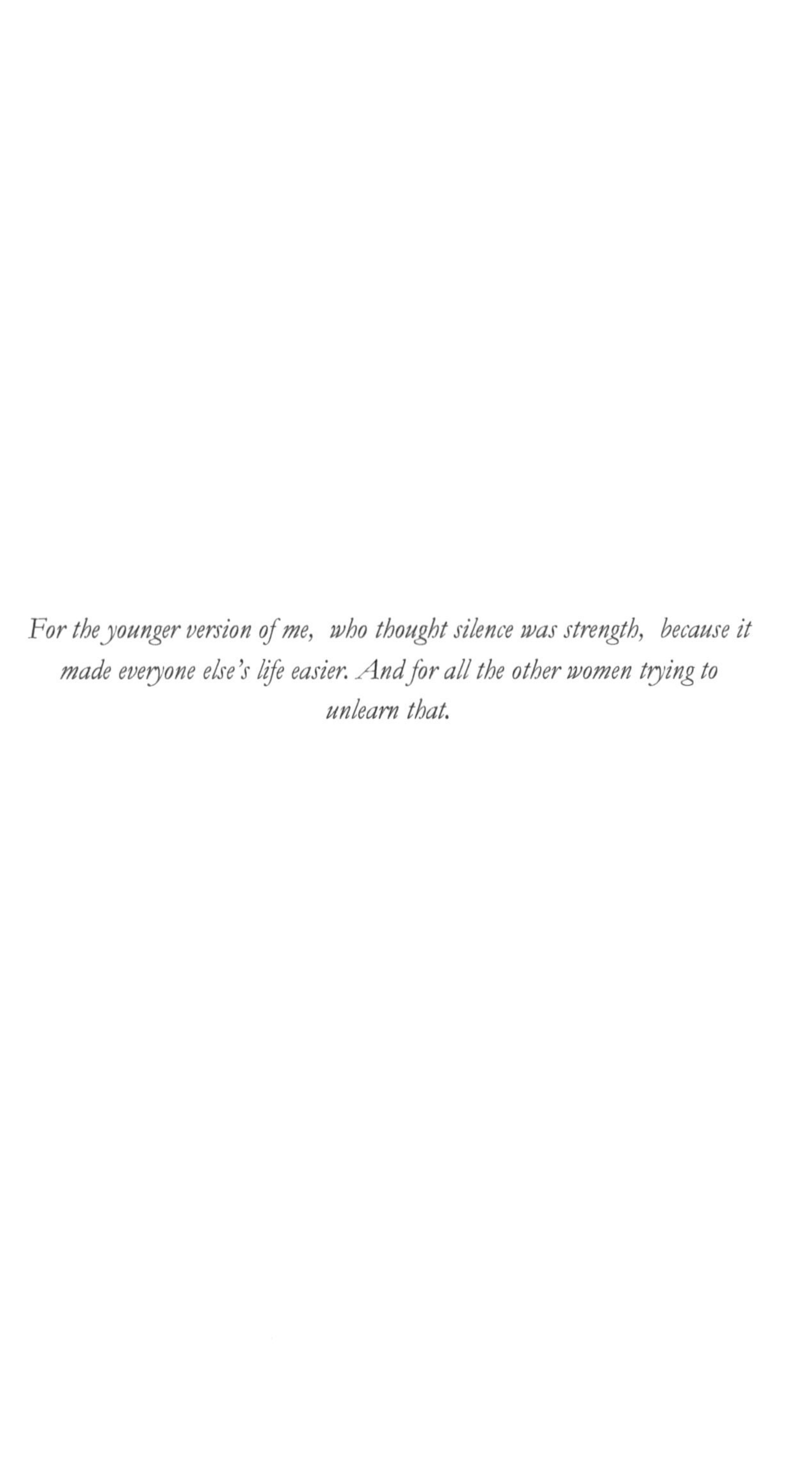

For the younger version of me, who thought silence was strength, because it made everyone else's life easier. And for all the other women trying to unlearn that.

It Gets Better

Contents

Chapter One Introduction

I AM A LOT OF THINGS. A mixed bag of trauma and sarcasm, if we're being honest. Life has a way of shaping you like that when you've known loss the way I have. I've lost innocence. I've lost pieces of my family. I've lost children, in more than one way. And those kinds of losses don't just pass through you. They settle in, take root, and quietly rearrange who you are.

But this book isn't about all of that.

Because to tell every one of those stories would mean going back to versions of myself I worked really hard to survive, and I can't do that—not without losing sight of what I hope this becomes. This book isn't about who I was back then. It's about who I am now. Someone who knows what it feels like to be surrounded by people who care and still feel completely, painfully alone.

Loss has touched my life in a lot of ways, but the thing that set all of this in motion, the thing that gave this book its voice, was my son, Jaxon, who I lost seventeen years ago. For a long time after he was born, I didn't just grieve him. I grieved in silence. Not because no one wanted to be there, but because the people who could be there didn't know how. And if I'm being fair, neither did I. We were all trying to navigate something none of us understood.

But somewhere in that space, in all the attempts to help, something else happened. The words people offered—well-meaning, kind, intended to comfort—often landed in ways that hurt more than they healed. At the time, I didn't fully recognize it. I was too deep in it, too busy trying to survive each day to examine why certain things lingered the way they did.

I'm in a different place now. I'm surrounded by love and support, and I can see more clearly what I couldn't then. But there was a time when I came dangerously close to losing myself entirely in that grief, when the weight of it felt like it might pull me under for good. It's taken me nearly two decades to find the words for that experience, to untangle what hurt, what helped, and what quietly made everything harder.

And that's why this book exists.

I hope it helps grieving mothers feel seen in a way they might not have felt before, to recognize themselves in these pages and feel, even for a moment, less alone in something that can feel impossibly isolating. And at the same time, I hope it helps the people who love them feel more equipped to show up in a way that actually matters. Because most people want to help. They don't always know how. And sometimes, without meaning to, the words they choose can carry a weight they never intended.

You might be wondering who I am to say any of this, and that's a fair question. I'm not a psychiatrist or a psychologist. I don't have years of professional training or research to back me up. I'm not an authority on grief, and I'm not here to speak for every mother who has experienced loss.

I'm just a mother who has lived it.

A mother who has felt the emptiness that follows losing a child, and the pressure of the world around her as it waits for her to be okay again. I was introduced to a kind of grief I didn't know existed and to a world full of people trying their best to say the right thing, even when those words didn't land the way they'd hoped.

I spent a long time wishing someone had told me the truth. That there is no right way to grieve. There is no timeline, no moment when it suddenly resolves into something manageable. There is no magic fix-it button. There is only the slow, uneven process of learning how to carry something that never really gets lighter.

More than anything, I wish someone had just looked at me and said, "This fucking sucks." And then stayed.

So I guess what I'm trying to do with this book is to be your "Fuck This" person if you need one. The person who doesn't look away. The one who doesn't try to soften it into something more comfortable than it is. The one who is willing to sit in the truth of it, even when that truth is messy and sharp and hard to hold.

The reality is, there is no universal playbook for supporting someone through grief. What comforts one person might hurt another. What feels helpful one day might feel unbearable the next. It's not something you can solve or fix. It's just something you have to be willing to witness.

At its core, supporting someone through loss is about knowing the person in front of you and being willing to meet them exactly where they are, without trying to move them somewhere else.

What I offer here is perspective. Mine, and the voices of other mothers I've spoken to along the way. Women who have experienced loss in different forms: miscarriage, stillbirth, infancy, childhood, adolescence, even adulthood. We are not separated by how much we loved our children, only by how long we were given to love them.

This book is a collection of the things people say when they're trying to help, and how those words can actually land. My intention is not to shame or judge, but to offer a different way of understanding. Because intention and impact are not always the same, and grief has a way of amplifying that gap.

Alongside those phrases, I'll offer something else: alternatives. Not perfect scripts or rehearsed lines, but ways of showing up that don't rely on saying the exact right thing. Sometimes, when you don't know what to say, it really is better to say nothing at all.

And if you feel like you have to say something, let it be this: I'm here.

That's it.

That's enough.

I didn't learn what helps from someone sitting me down and teaching me. I learned it by hearing everything that didn't. By sitting there, nodding along, while something inside me quietly broke a little more each time someone tried to say the right thing. At the time, I couldn't always explain why it hurt. I just knew that it did, and that knowing without understanding made it harder to process, not easier. It's only now, years later, that I can finally put words to those moments, to trace back where they landed and why they stayed. And maybe that's the point of this book—not to rewrite those experiences, but to finally make sense of them.

I know this book won't resonate with everyone. Some of it may not apply to you. Some of it might even bring comfort in a way it never did for me. And that's okay. Grief isn't one-size-fits-all, and neither is support.

But if even one person reads this and feels a little less alone, or if it helps someone show up more fully for someone they love, then it was worth writing.

Chapter Two
Early Days

The Days After

THERE'S A STRANGE STILLNESS IN the days after loss, but it isn't the kind of stillness you expect. It isn't quiet because the world pauses with you. It's quiet because everything keeps going without you. People talk. Phones ring. Conversations continue as if nothing has shifted. Life moves forward in ways that feel almost offensive, like something this big should have changed everything, and instead, nothing looks different at all.

And you're just… there.

Existing in a moment that doesn't make sense, trying to orient yourself in a reality that no longer feels recognizable.

I remember feeling like the world should have stopped, like something this devastating should have been enough to interrupt everything. It felt like there should have been some visible shift, some sign that what had happened mattered beyond those walls. But it didn't. The sun still came up. People still laughed. Cars still drove by as if nothing had changed. And I remember thinking, over and over, how is that possible? How can everything look exactly the same when nothing feels the same?

Grief like this doesn't move gently. It doesn't give you time to adjust. It feels like drowning, like coming up for air just long enough to breathe before you're pulled under again. Again and again, without rhythm, without warning. There's no pattern to it, no way to prepare for when it will hit or how hard it will pull you down. It just does.

And then there are the firsts, because everything that comes after loss becomes defined by them. The first time you leave the hospital. The first time you go home. The first time you understand that this isn't temporary, that there is no version of this where things go back to what they were.

I remember being discharged at the same time as another mother. We were both standing there, waiting for our cars, close enough to see each other clearly, but existing in completely different realities. She was holding her baby, adjusting the blanket, completely absorbed in a moment that should have felt ordinary. And my arms were empty.

Not only empty in the sense that I wasn't holding anything, but empty in a way that felt wrong, like something that should have been there wasn't. My body still expected the weight of him, the instinct to hold, to adjust, to protect—except there was nothing there to hold.

For a second, I felt something sharp and immediate. I thought I hated her. Not because she had done anything wrong, and not because she didn't deserve that moment, but because she had what I wanted so badly that it hurt to see. The feeling passed quickly, replaced by something I could better understand. It wasn't about her. I would never wish this on anyone. I just wanted what she had, and I couldn't have it.

I had spent days on the postpartum floor hearing babies cry, hearing parents celebrate, listening to the sounds of lives beginning all around me. And now I was watching them leave, stepping into something full of hope, full of joy, carrying their babies out into a world that was ready for them.

And I was standing there with a small purple box.

A hat. A blanket. A tiny bracelet that said *Jaxon.*

That's what I was taking home.

And that feeling? That's what people don't see. They see the moment it happens. They see the initial grief, the shock, the heartbreak that is visible and immediate. But they don't see the days after, when everything quiets down and the world keeps moving forward, and you're left trying to figure out how to exist in something that doesn't make sense—and never will.

"You should..."

In the days and weeks that follow loss, people start trying to help. They offer suggestions—things to do, ways to cope, ideas that might give you something to hold onto. And I understand why. When something feels this overwhelming, the instinct is to reach for anything that looks like relief. People want to do something. They want to offer a solution to something that feels completely unsolvable.

But grief isn't something you fix.

And in those early days, there is no distraction strong enough to take that kind of pain away. No hobby that softens it. No routine that makes it manageable. Because this isn't a momentary sadness; it's deep and strong. And the only thing a newly grieving mother should be doing is surviving.

That might look like eating when she can, sleeping when she can, getting through one hour at a time without completely unraveling. It might not look like anything at all from the outside.

There is no productivity requirement in grief. There is no expectation to turn it into something meaningful or to channel it into something useful. Distraction doesn't heal it; it just delays it. And eventually, it finds you again, often when you least expect it.

That doesn't mean these suggestions are always wrong, but timing matters. Later, when the grief isn't so raw, when there's a little more space between the waves, those things can help *if* they come from a place of knowing her, of understanding what actually brings her comfort.

There's a difference between offering and instructing. Between saying, "I know you love this… maybe it could help a little," and saying, "You should do this."

One feels like support. The other feels like pressure.

And a grieving mother doesn't need instructions. She needs space—space to feel what she's already carrying without being asked to reshape it, manage it, or move through it any faster than she can.

What you might have meant:

"I want to help you feel even a little bit better."
"I don't know what to do, but I want to offer something."
"I'm trying to give you something to hold onto."

What you could have said instead:

"You don't have to do anything right now."
"I'm here with you."
"If you ever want a distraction, I'm here for that too."

There will be time for hobbies. Time for distractions. Time for figuring out what helps. But in the beginning, she doesn't need something to do. She needs the room to feel what she's already carrying.

"It gets better."

"It gets better."

"It will get easier."

"Eventually you'll move on."

"It won't hurt this much forever."

I understand why people say this. I really do. When someone you care about is in pain, your instinct is to reach for something hopeful, something that suggests relief is coming, something that reassures them that this feeling won't last forever. It's an attempt to offer a future where things feel lighter, more manageable, less overwhelming.

But grief like this doesn't work that way. It doesn't get easier, and it doesn't hurt less. What changes—over time—is you.

You learn how to live with it. You learn how to carry it in a way that doesn't completely take you under every single day. You learn how to exist in a world that kept moving when a piece of yours stopped. The pain doesn't shrink or fade into something distant; it becomes something you live alongside, something woven into your everyday life in ways that are both subtle and constant.

That doesn't mean your life is over or that you are always consumed by sadness. You still laugh. You still celebrate. You still experience moments that are full and meaningful and real.

Life continues, whether you feel ready for it or not. But it continues with something extra.

There is a quiet, constant awareness that someone is missing from it. You feel it in the small moments more than the big ones, in the pauses between conversations, in the spaces where something should be but isn't. Every holiday carries a gap that wasn't there before. Every family photo holds an absence you can feel, even if no one else notices it. Every milestone with your other children is beautiful but layered, because alongside the pride and joy there is a thought that never quite leaves you:

"I wonder what he would have done?"

That question becomes part of your everyday thinking. It settles into the way you experience life, shaping moments in ways that are hard to explain to anyone who hasn't lived it.

Seventeen years later, I still think of him every day. Not always in a way that stops everything or pulls me under, but in quieter, steadier ways. He exists in the background of my life now, in the in-between spaces where memory lives.

And I want to be clear about something, because this part matters.

My life did not end. I am not stuck in grief. I have joy. I have laughter. I have moments that are beautiful and true. But even in those moments, there is something that changes them. As wonderful as those moments are, there is always a part of me that knows they would be even better if he were here.

There's a version of my life that exists alongside the one I'm living. Not in some dramatic, larger-than-life way, but in the small, ordinary details. What he would have been like. The way he would have fit into our family. The sound of his voice. The shape of his presence in a life that continued without him.

I carry both versions at the same time: the life I have and the one I don't.

That's the part people don't understand when they say it gets easier. They imagine a future where the pain fades, where it softens into something distant, where you eventually move on. But you don't move on from your child. You move forward with their memory—with the love, with the loss, with both versions of your life existing side by side.

It doesn't get easier. It becomes familiar. And familiar doesn't mean small; it means you've learned how to carry it without it breaking you every single day.

What you might have meant:

"I don't want you to feel like this forever."
"I hope you find moments where it feels lighter."
"I want to believe life will hold something good for you again."

What you could have said instead:

"I'm here for you, now and later."
"You don't have to rush your grief."
"I'm not going anywhere."

Grief isn't something you get through; it's something you learn to live with. And living with it doesn't make it smaller. It just means you've grown around it.

"At least…"

"At least you have other children."

"At least they're in a better place."

"At least you got some time with them."

"At least they aren't suffering."

If a sentence meant to comfort someone starts with "at least," it probably won't land the way you hope it will. The intention behind it is almost always good. People are trying to find something, anything, that might make the situation feel a little less devastating, something that introduces even the smallest sense of balance into a situation that feels overwhelmingly unfair.

But "at least" doesn't comfort. It compares and minimizes. It takes something immeasurable and tries to reshape it into something that feels more manageable from the outside. And grief doesn't respond to that kind of logic. It doesn't soften because you've pointed out something that could be worse. It doesn't become easier to carry because there is something else in the picture that is good.

There is no "at least" when it comes to losing a child. It doesn't matter how old they were, how much time you had, or what the circumstances were. The loss is still the loss, and it exists on its own terms. When you try to attach an "at least" to it, it often feels like an attempt to make it more acceptable, to round the edges of something that cannot be rounded.

When someone says, "at least they aren't suffering," what they may mean is that the child is no longer in pain and there is some form of peace in that. Maybe, in an abstract or logical way, that idea brings comfort to the person saying it.

But a parent doesn't experience their child as a concept. They experience them as theirs. The absence of suffering does not make the absence of your child easier to carry. It doesn't replace the physical, emotional, and lived reality of them not being here. It simply means you are now holding a different kind of pain, one that doesn't come with answers or resolve into something easier to accept.

When someone says, "At least you have other children," it often feels like a redirection. A suggestion to focus on what remains instead of what's missing, as if one can somehow offset the other.

So let me say this clearly.

I love my children. Deeply. Fully. Completely. They bring joy into my life every single day. There is real happiness. There is laughter, connection, and moments that are worth everything.

And none of that—not one piece of that—makes their brother not being here acceptable.

Loving them does not cancel out missing him. It doesn't balance it. It doesn't soften it. Those experiences exist alongside each other, not in opposition, and not in a way that evens out. There is no trade-off. There is no version of this where one makes the other okay. Because that's what "at least" tries to do, whether you intend it to or not. It tries to tip the scale. It tries to say: yes, this is terrible, but look at this over here. And there is no "but" big enough.

When someone says, "at least you got some time with them," it can sound like an attempt to frame the loss as something partially fulfilled, as if having some time makes the ending more acceptable. But no amount of time with your child ever feels enough. There is no version of this where a parent looks back and thinks, yes, that was sufficient.

"At least" statements don't take away pain. They try to reshape it into something that feels more balanced, more explainable, more tolerable to the person observing it. But this isn't something that balances. This isn't a trade.

Grief doesn't cancel out joy, and joy doesn't cancel out grief. Both can exist at the same time without diminishing each other. I can love the life I have. I can feel genuine happiness in the moments I'm living. I can laugh, celebrate, and be present with the people who are here.

And at the exact same time, I can mourn the fact that my son is not part of it. I can hold both. Not as opposites, but as realities that exist side by side.

And that's where "at least" falls apart, because it tries to resolve something that cannot be resolved. It tries to answer a question that doesn't have an answer, to fill a space that cannot be filled. Because every happy moment still carries a quiet question underneath it:

"What would this have looked like if he were here?"

And no "at least" will ever be enough to answer that. There is no version of this where losing your child becomes acceptable. There is no version where it becomes worth it, or understandable, or balanced out by something else that exists alongside it.

The idea that something good could make this loss make sense isn't comforting. It's impossible.

What you might have meant:

"I don't want this to feel as devastating as it is."
"I'm trying to find something, anything, that might bring you comfort."
"I don't know how to sit in this with you."

What you could have said instead:

"I'm so sorry."
"I can't imagine how much you miss them."
"Tell me about them."

You don't need to soften someone's grief to support them. You don't need to compare it or try to balance it into something more manageable. Sometimes the most compassionate thing you can do is allow the loss to be exactly what it is, without trying to follow it with something that makes it easier to accept.

"Be strong."

"Be strong."

"Stay strong."

"You have to be strong for your family."

This is one of those things people say that sounds right. It sounds supportive, even encouraging, like they're trying to remind you that you can get through this, that you have something inside you that will carry you forward.

But grief doesn't hear it that way.

When you tell a grieving parent to be strong, it often sounds like: Don't fall apart. Don't let this take you down. Hold it together. And the truth is, losing a child is the kind of thing that should break you.

Not permanently, and not in a way that means you'll never stand again, but in a way that reflects the magnitude of what just happened. This is not a small loss that can be managed quietly or carried neatly. It is a rupture. It changes the structure of everything.

And this is where people get it backwards. Losing a child is not the time for a family to be strong. It's the time they fall apart.

When people say, "be strong for each other," it sounds like they're asking parents to hold each other up, to take turns carrying the weight so neither one collapses. But in reality, both people are already collapsing under the same weight. They are grieving the same loss, even if it shows up differently, and asking one to be strong for the other doesn't lighten that load. It redistributes it.

This becomes even more complicated when that expectation is directed at fathers.

"Be strong for her."

As if strength is something he is supposed to provide while she falls apart, as if his role is to stabilize everything instead of experiencing what he has just lost. But he just lost his child, too. His grief may not look the same, but it is just as real, just as deep, and just as deserving of space.

Telling him to be strong for her doesn't support her. It takes something away from him.

It tells him that his pain comes second, that his role is to manage instead of to feel. And that isn't fair. Neither of them should have to carry that alone, and neither of them should be asked to suppress what they are experiencing for the sake of appearing strong.

This is the one time they shouldn't be strong for each other. They should fall apart together. They should sit in it together, without expectation, without roles, without one person being responsible for holding the other up. Because they are the only two people who understand that exact loss in that exact way.

The strength should not be coming from within the family that just broke. It should come from the people around them. From the ones standing just outside the center of that loss, who are not carrying it in the same way, but who can help hold everything steady while nothing inside feels steady at all. That is what support is supposed to look like.

There is an unspoken expectation that grief should be handled with grace, that it should be carried in a way that looks composed, dignified, and controlled. But there is nothing neat or controlled about losing a child. It is disorienting, overwhelming, and deeply human in the way it breaks through whatever structure you thought you had.

You don't owe anyone a polished version of your grief.

You don't owe anyone strength that looks good from the outside.

Because here's the truth: you are already strong. You are strong in ways you never asked to be, strong in ways that were forced onto you, strong in ways that don't feel like strength at all. You don't need to prove it, and you don't need to perform it for anyone else's comfort.

What you need is space—space to fall apart without being told to hold it together, space to feel what you feel without being asked to package it into something more manageable. Grief doesn't require strength from the people experiencing it, especially in the beginning. It requires the support of the people around them, the ones who can hold them up while they are falling, who can steady things when nothing feels steady.

What you might have meant:

"I believe in you."
"I don't want to see you fall apart."
"I wish I could take some of this from you."

What you could have said instead:

"You don't have to be strong right now."
"You can fall apart here."
"I've got you."

And sometimes, the strongest thing a person can do is stop trying to hold everything together and allow someone else to hold it for a while.

Thoughts From Other Mothers

Over time, I've come to understand that while loss connects us, grief does not look the same for any two people who experience it. The details are different. The circumstances are different. The way it shows up, the way it settles in, the way it changes you—all of that is deeply personal.

There are threads that run through it, things that feel familiar when you hear someone else speak about their loss, but there is no single version of grief that fits everyone. No universal way to carry it. No one experience that can speak for all of us.

And that matters.

I never want this book to feel like I'm telling you: this is what grief is, or this is how it feels, as if my experience is the only one that exists. It isn't. It's just mine.

There are so many mothers out there who carry this in their own way, who have their own stories, their own moments, their own words for something that often feels impossible to explain. And their voices deserve space here too. So throughout this book, I'll be including reflections from other mothers: women with different experiences, different perspectives, but connected by something we all understand in our own way.

This is one of those voices.

Diana M.

Oh gosh... where do I begin? I think for me the worst ones were, "at least you know you can still get pregnant," or "you can always try again," along with the ones you listed. Jeff and I didn't have the luxury of getting pregnant easily. Hell, it took us five years for us to even conceive our first child together. Getting pregnant was never easy for us; I wasn't a fertile myrtle.

After our miscarriage in 2019, we took a few years to really evaluate if we wanted more kids. Once we decided we wanted to try again, it took us another two and a half years to conceive again. Finding the right things to say is always hard, sometimes just being present and providing a safe space for the grieving parents to feel what they want to feel and say what they want to say helps more than people know.

Whether it's saying that they're angry at God for what happened (I know I was), allowing them to question their faith, saying why me? Just things like that.

Chapter Three
The External World

Secondary Losses

AT THE TIME I LOST HIM, I was already in a very raw and transitional place in my life. I was in the middle of something that had already begun to unravel who I thought I was, quietly pulling apart the version of myself I had always known. And then I lost him.

Before losing him, I was already letting go of everything I thought I was. With his passing, I also lost everything I thought I was going to be. I lost my son, and somewhere inside that, I lost myself too.

It didn't happen all at once. There wasn't a single moment when I could point and say, "That's when I disappeared." It happened gradually, in ways that were easy to miss from the outside. I stopped trusting that anything good would last. I pulled back from people without always realizing I was doing it. I forgot what it felt like to hope for something without immediately bracing for it to be taken away.

Somewhere along the way, I convinced myself that I was no longer worth being loved, and once I believed that, I started to act like it was true. I pushed people away. I shut down when they got too close. I made it difficult, sometimes intentionally, sometimes without even knowing I was doing it. It felt safer that way, as if creating the distance first meant I wouldn't have to feel it when it inevitably happened anyway.

But some people didn't listen. They stayed anyway.

They stayed through the distance, through the silence, through all the ways I tried to make myself smaller and harder to reach. They loved me through it, even when I made it difficult, even when I gave them every reason to leave. And I am so grateful for them because I don't know what version of me would exist now if they had let me disappear.

This is a part people don't really talk about—the secondary losses.

The way your entire world shifts, not just around you, but inside you. Your identity changes, and your sense of self reshapes itself around something you never asked to carry. And for parents like me, those losses aren't always obvious to other people.

When someone loses a spouse, there are visible ripples. There may be a loss of income, changes in living situations, shifts in routine—things people can point to and say, "This is what was lost." And those losses are real. They deserve to be seen.

But mine weren't visible in the same way.

Losing my son before he had the chance to live didn't create those same tangible changes. I wasn't grieving a routine that had already taken shape or a life that had fully unfolded. I was grieving something harder to name—a future I would never get to see, a person I would never get to know.

And that kind of loss doesn't show up in obvious ways, but it still ripples. It shows up in the absence of memories that never had the chance to exist, in the questions that don't have answers, in the quiet awareness of something that should have been there but isn't. Even now, I don't look at situations and know what he would have done. I don't have stories to pull from or memories to revisit. Instead, I have questions, endless ones that don't resolve into anything solid.

I find myself playing out scenarios in my head, over and over, trying to fill in something that was never given the chance to exist. Who he would have been, what he would have loved, what kind of person he would have grown into.

I don't have those answers, so I create them. Not just one version, but many. Different possibilities, different lives, different versions of him that exist only in my imagination. None of them real, but all of them his in the only way I have left.

And that's a loss people don't always see—not just who you lost, but everything that was supposed to come with them.

"They would want you to be happy."

"They would want you to be happy."

"They wouldn't want you to be sad like this."

"You know they'd want you to keep living your life."

These are the kinds of things people say when they don't know what to do with someone else's grief. They reach for something that sounds hopeful and suggests there's a way forward, even if no one is quite sure what that looks like yet.

But when this is said to a grieving parent, especially in the early days when everything still feels raw and unreal, it doesn't land as comforting. It feels like pressure to move on before they are ready. Like there is a right way to move through this, and maybe you're already falling behind.

And if you follow the logic all the way through, it starts to fall apart. No mother is going to hear, "They would want you to be happy," and suddenly think, "You know what, you're right! I've been devastated long enough. Let's go to Disney."

That kind of shift doesn't happen on command because happiness and grief don't operate on the same timeline, and they don't cancel each other out. Loving your child doesn't mean skipping over your sadness for their sake. It means allowing yourself to feel it fully, without editing it down to make other people more comfortable.

When someone says, "They wouldn't want you to be sad," what often comes through is the idea that this level of grief is too much, or lasting too long, or that it would be better to start moving toward something lighter. But grief follows its own pace, and it doesn't respond to suggestions about where it should go next. The sadness isn't a problem to solve. It reflects the depth of the relationship, the weight of what was lost, and the reality that something irreplaceable is no longer here.

No one is choosing to stay in that space. No one wakes up and decides to feel this way. They are living inside something that doesn't have a clear path through it, something that unfolds in its own time whether anyone is comfortable with it or not.

And if we're going to apply this idea consistently, then let me add a personal note…

To everyone who loves me: if I die suddenly, I do not want or expect you to be happy in that moment. I hope you get there eventually, but I fully expect dramatic tears. And especially you, husband. You should be at least a little ruined for any other woman for a while.

Because that's what love looks like.

It shows up in the grief. It shows up in the absence. It shows up in the way someone is missed long after they're gone. Expecting someone to move quickly past that doesn't honor the relationship; it forces them to a point they aren't ready to face.

There is a difference between wanting someone to be okay someday and expecting them to be okay right now. Those two things often get blurred together, but they are not the same.

Over time, happiness does find its way back in. Not as a replacement for grief, but alongside it. That shift doesn't happen because someone was reminded it should. It happens because there was enough space to feel everything honestly, without pressure, without timelines, and without someone trying to redirect it into something easier to witness.

What you might have meant:

"I don't want you to stay in this pain forever."
"I want you to find moments where life feels good again."
"I care about you, and I want you to be okay."

What you could have said instead:

"You don't have to rush this."
"I'm here with you, however this looks."
"You can feel all of this."

Grief doesn't take anything away from love. If anything, it shows exactly how much of it was there to begin with, and sometimes the most honest way that love shows up is in how deeply someone is missed.

"I know exactly how you feel."

That phrase is almost always meant to comfort. It comes from a place of wanting to connect, of wanting to close the distance between you and someone who is hurting. But even when it's well-intentioned, it doesn't land the way people hope it will.

Because the truth is, you don't know.

And that isn't said to be harsh. It's said because grief doesn't exist in a way that can be fully shared or replicated. Even if you have experienced loss, even if you have lost a child, your experience is still your own. It is shaped by who your child was, who you are, the life you built around them, and the future you imagined with them in it.

No two people carry grief the same way, even when the loss itself looks similar from the outside. When someone says, "I know exactly how you feel," it can sometimes take something deeply personal and flatten it into something more general. It shifts the moment from being about the person who is grieving to something that now includes your experience too, even if that wasn't the intention.

And in a moment like that, the difference matters. Because this isn't just grief in a broad sense. It's their grief, theirs in a way that cannot be duplicated or wholly understood from the outside. Trying to match it, even gently, can unintentionally take something away from that.

At the same time, the instinct behind the phrase makes sense. If you have experienced loss, especially something as profound as losing a child, there is a natural pull to reach out and say, you are not alone in this. There is a desire to offer proof that someone else has survived it, that there is a version of life that continues, even if it looks different.

But connection doesn't require comparison.

It doesn't require placing your story alongside theirs or finding the overlap between the two. In fact, doing that too quickly can shift the focus away from what they are feeling and toward how it relates to you, even in subtle ways.

There is another way to show up, one that doesn't require you to fully understand what they are experiencing in order to stand beside them.

Instead of trying to define their grief, you can acknowledge that you don't fully know what it feels like and remain present anyway. That kind of presence leaves room for their experience to exist without being shaped or interpreted.

If they ask about your story, if they open that door, then you can share. You can talk about what helped you, what didn't, what you learned along the way. But even then, the center of the conversation stays with them, because in that moment, it isn't about your loss.

It's about where they are right now. And if you haven't experienced this kind of loss, this becomes even more important. The urge to compare it to something familiar can be strong, but those comparisons often create more distance than connection. Not every loss is the same, and trying to make them equivalent can leave a grieving parent feeling misunderstood rather than supported.

That doesn't mean you should stay silent. Silence can hurt too. Disappearing because you don't know what to say can feel like being left alone in the worst moment of someone's life. Reaching out still matters.

What changes is how you do it. You don't need perfect words. You don't need shared experience. You don't need to fully understand.

You just need to show up in a way that keeps the focus on them, allowing their grief to be exactly what it is without trying to reshape it into something more familiar or easier to relate to.

What you might have meant:

"You're not alone in this."
"I want you to know someone else has survived something similar."
"I don't know how to help, but I want to connect with you."

What you could have said instead:

"I can't imagine how you're feeling, but I'm here."
"You don't have to go through this alone."
"I'm here to listen."

You don't have to know exactly how someone feels to care about them. Sometimes the most meaningful thing you can do is acknowledge that you don't—and stay present anyway.

"I don't know what I would do if it were me."

I know what I would do if it were you… I would stop talking.

That thought isn't coming from a place of anger, even if it sounds sharp. It comes from understanding what that moment actually needs—and what it doesn't.

This phrase is usually meant to show empathy. It's someone trying to acknowledge how overwhelming the situation is, how unimaginable it feels from the outside. It's an attempt to say, "This is bigger than anything I can comprehend." But what it actually does is shift the focus.

Instead of staying with her grief, the conversation moves toward you—what you would do, how you would feel, how you can't imagine surviving something like this. And while that might feel like connection from your side, it can land differently for the person living it.

Because she didn't get the option of not imagining it. She's living it.

So when someone says they don't know what they would do, what can come through underneath that is something else entirely. It can sound like, "I wouldn't be able to handle this," or "I couldn't survive something like this." And she is standing there, already doing exactly that.

Not because she is stronger than you. Not because she is built differently. But because she doesn't have a choice.

And there's something exhausting about that moment because now, on top of everything she is already carrying, she is also being asked, implicitly, to hold your reaction to it. She may find herself reassuring you, softening your discomfort, or responding in a way that protects your feelings.

Even here, even now, she is still taking care of other people. And she just lost her child. It is not her job to comfort you.

There is also a deeper misconception underneath this phrase—that a grieving mother *wants* you to fully understand her pain, to imagine yourself in her position so you can meet her there.

She doesn't.

No one who has lived through this wants someone else to understand it by experiencing it themselves. This is not something anyone wishes to share in that way. You don't need to feel it as deeply as she does in order to show up for her. You can sit beside her in it without carrying it the same way. Because what she needs is not for you to understand her pain completely. She needs you to acknowledge that it exists, and to stay.

When someone says they can't imagine it and then instinctively pulls back from that discomfort, it can leave her more alone than she already was. It creates distance at a moment when presence is needed most.

And that's the part that matters.

Not whether you can imagine it. But whether you're willing to stay.

What you might have meant:

"This is unimaginable."
"I can't comprehend this kind of pain."
"My heart breaks for you."

What you could have said instead:

"I don't have words for this, but I'm here."
"I'm so sorry."
"You don't have to go through this alone."

You don't need to put yourself in her place to support her. You just need to stand beside her in the one she's already in.

"It didn't have to be this way."

"It didn't have to be this way."

"They should have done more."

"There must have been signs."

These are the kinds of things people say when they are trying to make sense of something that doesn't make sense. They are looking for a reason, for a point where something could have gone differently, for a version of the story where the ending changes into something easier to accept.

But for a grieving mother, that process has already begun long before anyone else speaks it out loud.

Those thoughts don't need to be introduced. They are already there, moving quietly in the background, replaying themselves in ways that are difficult to interrupt. Every decision gets revisited. Every moment gets reexamined. The mind searches for something, anything, that might explain how things unfolded the way they did because having no explanation at all feels unbearable.

It isn't a single question. It becomes a pattern of thinking that circles back on itself: wondering whether something was missed, whether something could have been noticed sooner, whether a different decision or a different response might have changed the outcome. Even when those questions don't lead anywhere, they don't simply disappear. They linger.

And there is a difference between a mother choosing to share those thoughts and someone else placing them there.

When statements like "It didn't have to be this way," or "There must have been signs," are said out loud, they don't provide clarity. Instead, they give more weight to something that is already heavy. They take thoughts that may have been internal, uncertain, and difficult to articulate, and make them feel more defined, more concrete, and therefore harder to set down.

Because at the center of all those questions, whether they are spoken or not, is a place many mothers eventually arrive.

They look inward.

Not because it is logical, and not because it is true, but because of something deeper, something instinctive. At the core of motherhood is the belief that you are meant to protect your child. When something happens that you could not prevent, that belief doesn't simply disappear. It turns into a search for where that protection failed.

The way that shows up depends on the circumstances, but the pattern is the same. A loss during pregnancy or birth can lead to the feeling that the body itself failed. Illness can turn into questions about genetics or missed signs. Suicide can bring an overwhelming sense that something should have been seen or understood sooner. Loss caused by someone else can lead to the belief that there should have been a way to prevent it.

Even when none of those conclusions are grounded in reality, they still take hold. Even when there is no logical reason to assign blame, the mind continues to look for it. Having nowhere to place that responsibility can feel even more unsettling than placing it in the wrong place.

So when someone outside that grief begins to point toward all the ways things could have gone differently, it doesn't bring relief. It reinforces the very thing that is already happening internally—the quiet, persistent question of whether this could have been prevented.

That is why these statements matter.

Not because they are intentionally harmful, but because they add to something that is already in motion. They add more "what ifs" to a mind that is already full of them.

Grief does not need more questions. It does not need investigation or analysis, and it does not need someone trying to reconstruct a version of the story where the ending is different.

Because that version does not exist. And continuing to search for it only deepens the pain.

What you might have meant:

"This feels unfair."
"I wish this hadn't happened."
"I'm trying to make sense of something that doesn't make sense."

What you could have said instead:

"I'm so sorry this happened."
"This wasn't your fault."
"I'm here with you."

You don't need to help a grieving mother find answers. The hardest questions are already living in her head. What she needs instead is a safe environment for her grief, one where those questions are not made louder, and where, over time, she might begin to loosen her grip on the idea that any of this was hers to carry.

Thoughts From Other Mothers

The voices included in this book come from many different places.

Some of these mothers are people I have never met in person. Some I found in online spaces, in groups where loss brought us together in ways nothing else could. Others came into my life through friends or family connections—paths that might not have crossed otherwise, but did because of this shared experience.

And some of them are people I know deeply.

Women I have relationships with outside of this space, whose lives I have been a part of, and who have been a part of mine. The kind of relationships where you don't just witness someone's grief—you witness who they are inside it.

And I want to be honest about something here.

I have not always gotten it right.

There are moments, conversations, things I have said or done that I would handle differently now. Things I understand more clearly because of the work this book has required of me. Because of the listening. Because of the learning that came after the fact.

Julie is one of those people.

She is someone I care about deeply, and also someone I have learned from in ways that have shaped how I show up for others now. Watching the way she carries her grief and the way she continues to love the people around her—including people like me, who don't always say things perfectly—has been one of the most impactful lessons I've been given.

There is a kind of grace in that.

Not in the loss itself, but in the way she moves through it. In the way she makes space for other people's humanity, even when she is carrying something so heavy herself.

I'm incredibly grateful for her presence in my life and for what she has taught me—sometimes without even trying.

This is her voice.

Julie S.

When Max died, I knew I wasn't the only one grieving and feeling his loss. Not by a long shot. It's not a situation that one deals with on a regular basis so it really is a social unknown. I was very aware of people feeling helpless and wanting so badly to help find some way to ease our pain.

I've come to realize that faith in God and the passage of time are the only treatments for such grief. I gave family and friends a long leash, realizing they cared so much but felt so helpless. As a result, I took no offense to anything anyone said. No one ever intended any unkindness toward us. They just felt helpless. So, I accepted the love they were expressing over any verbal clumsiness. I was grateful for their presence and patient with their awkwardness.

Chapter Four 'Getting Over It'

The Moments No One Sees

GRIEF ISN'T ALWAYS LOUD.

It doesn't always look like crying, or breaking down, or not being able to function in ways that other people can recognize. Sometimes it looks like nothing at all. It looks like doing the dishes, folding laundry, or sitting in a room full of people and smiling at the right moments. From the outside, it blends in so seamlessly with everything else that there is no visible shift, no clear sign that anything is happening beneath the surface.

Most of the time, no one would know.

There are moments that belong only to me; small shifts that happen without warning and without witness. A thought that comes out of nowhere. A memory that surfaces in the middle of something completely ordinary. A brief pause where everything tilts just slightly, where something inside me changes in a way that is hard to explain but impossible to ignore. And then, just as quickly, I move through it and keep going.

Not because it's resolved, and not because it no longer matters, but because life keeps moving forward whether I'm ready for it or not. There are responsibilities, conversations, routines that don't pause to make space for what's happening internally, so I learn to carry it alongside everything else.

Some days, I carry it quietly, in a way that feels almost manageable. It sits just under the surface, not heavy enough to stop me, but never far enough away to forget. It moves with me throughout the day, present but contained, something I am aware of without it fully taking over.

Other times, it catches me off guard. A sound, a smell, or a thought that shouldn't mean anything suddenly does, and for a moment I am completely back there—fully in it, fully aware of everything that has been lost. It isn't gradual. It doesn't build slowly. It arrives all at once, and then, just as quickly, it recedes again.

From the outside, nothing changes. The conversation continues. The moment moves forward. The people around me stay exactly where they are, unaware that anything has shifted at all.

Not all grief asks to be witnessed, and not all of it announces itself in ways that are visible or easy to respond to. Some of it exists quietly in the middle of everything else, woven into the ordinary moments that continue whether you're ready for them or not.

Most of the time, I keep those moments to myself. Part of that is because sharing them often invites a response, something meant to help, to fix, or to redirect. Something that suggests I shouldn't still be carrying it this way, or that it would be better to let it go, as if grief follows a timeline that can be managed from the outside.

So instead, I hold onto them.

Not because they are small, but because they are mine. They belong to a part of my experience that doesn't always translate well into conversation, and I've learned that not everything needs to be explained in order to be real.

Living with grief has meant learning how to exist alongside it in this quieter form, not because it became easier, but because it became familiar. And familiarity doesn't take away the weight of it; it just means I've learned how to carry it without needing the world around me to stop every time it shows up.

"You have other kids to think about."

"You have other kids to think about."

"Think about your family."

Every year, without fail, around Jaxon's birthday, someone says it in one form or another. Sometimes it's gentle, sometimes it's more direct, but the message underneath it stays the same—a reminder that I still have other children who need me, and that my focus should be there. It's often offered as care, but it carries an assumption that taking time to acknowledge Jaxon somehow takes something away from my other children.

It doesn't.

Remembering my son or any of the children whom I lost before him in any way, has never reduced my love for my other children. If anything, it has reshaped that love in ways I didn't understand before. There is a sharper awareness now, a constant recognition of how fragile everything is and how quickly life can change. That awareness doesn't replace joy, but it sits alongside it, influencing how I move through ordinary moments that no longer feel ordinary.

Because of that, I love them differently.

I hold them closer. I pay attention in ways I might not have before. I notice the small things—the passing comments, the changing moods, the everyday interactions that might have felt routine but instead feel significant. That shift doesn't come from fear alone; it comes from knowing what it means to lose someone you love and understanding, in a way I wish I didn't, how quickly that can happen.

That understanding does not divide my love. It deepens it.

There is also something people don't always recognize about families like mine. Whether you had other children when your child died or you had more after, the child you lost does not stop being part of your family. They are not replaced, and they are not quietly removed from the story so that everything feels easier for the people who are still here. They remain part of how the family exists.

My children know they have siblings. I talk about them in ways they can understand, and they are allowed to ask questions and be curious about them. They also see that there are moments when I feel sad when I think about them, and that those moments are part of our life together, not something separate from it.

That part can make people uncomfortable. There is a common belief that children should be shielded from grief, that seeing a parent experience sadness is something harmful or destabilizing. The instinct behind that belief is protection, but in practice it can turn into avoidance, an effort to keep difficult emotions out of sight rather than helping children understand them.

What my children are seeing is not something damaging. They are seeing what love looks like when it continues after loss. They are learning that caring deeply about someone does not end when that person is gone, and that sadness is not something to be hidden or fixed, but something that can be felt and moved through. Emotions themselves are not the problem. Avoiding them is.

When someone tells a mother to focus on her other children, what is often being communicated, whether intentionally or not, is that this grief should be quieter, more contained, and less visible. The suggestion is that it should stay in the background so it doesn't interfere with what is still here.

But acknowledging one child does not take anything away from the others. Love doesn't work that way.

It doesn't divide itself based on who is present and who is not. It expands to hold all of it, the children who are here, and the ones who are missing. And when that space is allowed to exist, when all of those relationships are acknowledged instead of edited down, it does not weaken the family. It strengthens it.

What you might have meant:

"I don't want your other children to feel overlooked."
"I want to make sure you're supported in caring for your family."
"I don't know how to balance this, and I'm trying to help."

What you could have said instead:

"I see how much you love all of your children."
"I'm here for you, and your whole family."

You don't protect a family by pretending one of its members didn't exist. You protect it by making space for all of them, including the one who is missing.

"Everything happens for a reason."

"Everything happens for a reason."

The idea behind this is often presented as comfort. It suggests there is something beneath the surface of the loss that makes it make sense, something that gives the pain a purpose or a place to land. It introduces the possibility that, even if it doesn't feel clear right now, there is an explanation that will eventually make this easier to understand.

But when you are on the receiving end of that kind of loss, the question that follows is unavoidable.

What possible reason could exist that would make this make sense, and what explanation could ever make it feel acceptable?

Because what is being suggested, whether directly or indirectly, is that there is a purpose behind this. That this pain leads to something meaningful. That there is something, somewhere, that makes it worth it.

There isn't.

Losing a child does not feel like a lesson. It does not feel like growth or something that fits into a larger picture if you step back far enough. It feels like something has been taken in a way that cannot be replaced, like a space has been left that nothing else can fill. When people try to offer a reason for that loss, it can feel like they are trying to place something into that space, as if an explanation could somehow make it easier to carry.

It doesn't.

Even when it is said gently, it doesn't land differently. It might come with a softer tone or a sympathetic look, but the message underneath it stays the same—that this needed to happen, that there is something good that will come from it, that one day it will make sense. And for some people, that belief may feel comforting.

This is not about them. This is about what it feels like when it doesn't.

I don't want to understand this someday. I don't want clarity or perspective that allows me to look back and make peace with it in a way that turns it into something necessary. There is no version of understanding that makes losing a child acceptable, and there is no outcome that balances that kind of loss.

Sometimes the "reason" is reshaped into something that sounds more meaningful. That maybe this happened so you can help someone else through it.

But if the reason for my loss is to help someone else through theirs, and the reason for their loss is to help someone else, then this continues. It means more mothers will feel this. More families will live through this. More people will be forced into a version of life they never asked for.

There is nothing comforting about that. There is nothing meaningful about a system that builds purpose out of repeated suffering. And there is absolutely nothing that makes it easier to carry knowing that someone else will eventually feel the same kind of pain.

There is no version of this where that becomes meaningful. There is no version of this where that becomes okay. There is no version of this where that makes any sense.

That's not purpose. That's just more pain.

And if that's the "reason," then it's a fucking terrible one.

It doesn't make the loss meaningful. It doesn't make it easier to accept. It doesn't create purpose. It just spreads the pain. And while there is something deeply human about not wanting anyone to feel alone, no one wants you to understand this by living it. No one wants you to be part of something that exists because loss repeats itself over and over again.

Trying to assign meaning to that kind of suffering doesn't ease it. It builds something on top of it.

So when someone offers a reason, what it can feel like is not comfort, but an attempt to solve something that cannot be solved. It shifts the focus from acknowledging the loss to explaining it, as if explanation could somehow make it smaller or easier to carry. But this is not something that can be solved. It is something that has to be carried.

What you might have meant:

"I hate that this happened, and I don't know how to make it better."
"I wish there was a reason, because then maybe this wouldn't feel so unbearable."
"I want to give you something to hold onto."

What you could have said instead:

"This shouldn't have happened."
"I'm so sorry."
"I'm here."

You don't need a reason for your grief. You don't need your pain turned into something that makes sense to someone else. Sometimes things happen that are simply devastating, and the most compassionate thing you can do is acknowledge that reality instead of trying to explain it away.

Thoughts From Other Mothers

One of the things this book has made me realize is how much I didn't know, even about the people already in my life.

When I started writing, I expected to learn from strangers, from women I met in groups, in conversations that existed because of shared loss. And I have. But what I didn't expect was to discover how many people were already in my orbit who carried their own versions of this without ever speaking about it in a way I had truly heard.

Not because they were hiding it, but because I had never asked. That realization has stayed with me.

There were stories close to me that I hadn't heard, experiences that had shaped people in ways I hadn't fully seen. And that's something I've had to sit with, not in a way that is heavy with guilt, but in a way that makes me more aware of how I move through the people around me.

Maybe that's something I'm still learning.

That sometimes people don't need to be waiting for the right moment to share. Sometimes they need someone willing to ask, or at least willing to listen when the moment comes.

This is one of those perspectives.

Rachel C.

I experienced an early miscarriage this January, and one of the first things someone said to me was, "At least you already have three children. Be grateful for them."

And I am. I have always been grateful for each of my children, for how easily they came into our lives, for the privilege of being their mother. But gratitude and grief are not opposites. One does not cancel the other.

Secondary infertility/losses carry a quieter, more complicated kind of heartbreak. It comes when your home is already filled with children old enough to hope alongside you, children who ask for a baby brother or sister. It comes with the painful awareness that wanting something deeply does not mean you can make it happen.

When I told our oldest son about the miscarriage, he cried and cried. Watching his heartbreak unfold in front of me added a new layer to my own. In that moment, I felt like I had let him down too, as though my body had failed not just me, but my child who had already made space in his heart for someone we would never meet.

I was grieving a baby while trying to hold my child's grief at the same time, learning that loss doesn't belong to just one person. It ripples outward, touching every heart that dared to hope.

The most meaningful support didn't come from words meant to fix the pain, but from friends who simply let us grieve. The ones who sent care packages, checked in quietly, or sat with the sadness without trying to soften it. Sometimes the greatest kindness is not searching for the right thing to say, but choosing not to say the wrong thing at all.

Chapter Five
Getting Angry

Anger

IT'S OKAY TO BE ANGRY.

More than that, it's necessary. There is nothing fair about losing a child, nothing about it that makes sense, nothing that can be explained in a way that makes it easier. When something so permanent and life-altering happens without reason, without warning, without anything you can point to and say this is why, anger becomes part of how you process it.

For a long time, I was angry. Not at a person, and not at something I could clearly name or assign responsibility to. There wasn't a target for it, no single place to direct it. It existed more as a constant undercurrent, anger at the unfairness of it, at the fact that he was gone and the world kept moving as if nothing had changed, at the silence that followed, and at the words people used when they tried to make something unexplainable feel understandable.

And sometimes, those words gave that anger somewhere to go. When grief is handed explanations, especially ones tied to faith, purpose, or some kind of greater plan, it can shift that anger in a direction you weren't expecting. Instead of sitting in the loss itself, it can start to turn toward whatever higher power those explanations are rooted in. It creates questions you didn't ask for, and a tension between what you are being told to believe and what you are actually feeling. That's a complicated place to sit.

It wasn't loud anger. It didn't always look like yelling or breaking things or losing control in a way people would recognize. Most of the time, it showed up in more subtle ways. It felt like a tension that lived just under the surface, something I carried with me without always being able to name it in the moment. It showed up as thoughts I couldn't shake, as a tightness in my chest that had nowhere to go, as a feeling that stayed with me even when everything around me appeared normal.

And no one told me that was okay.

No one said, "You're allowed to be mad." No one gave me permission to feel that part of grief, so instead of recognizing it for what it was, I started to question it. That anger slowly turned into something else completely.

It turned into shame.

I convinced myself I wasn't grieving the "right" way, that I was supposed to be sad in a softer, more acceptable way. I thought grief was supposed to look gentle and contained, not sharp, not questioning, not filled with a sense that something had been taken from me that I should have been able to keep. But anger is part of it.

Love like that doesn't disappear quietly. It doesn't fade out in a way that feels neat or controlled. It pushes back. It demands answers. It looks for something, anything, that explains why this happened, even when there is no answer to be found.

And there is nothing wrong with that. There is nothing wrong with feeling angry about something that never should have happened. That anger is not a sign that something is wrong with you; it is a reflection of how deeply you loved and how significant that loss was.

You are not broken for feeling it. You are human.

And that anger does not make you a bad mother. If anything, it speaks to the depth of the bond that was there, to the reality of what was lost, and to the weight of continuing on without them.

I don't carry it the same way anymore. It doesn't sit as close to the surface as it once did, and it doesn't shape every moment the way it used to. But I don't regret it, because it was part of how I survived. It was part of how I moved through something that will never make sense, even now.

"It could be worse."

"It could be worse…"

This is often followed by examples—other ways children have died, other tragedies, other stories meant to put things into perspective. The intention is usually to soften the weight of what happened, to create some kind of framework where loss can be measured and compared in a way that feels more manageable.

But grief doesn't work that way. There is no scale that determines which loss hurts more and which one should hurt less. There is no ranking system where one version of this becomes easier to carry because something else might look worse from the outside. The idea that comparison can bring comfort assumes that grief is relative, that it can be adjusted depending on context.

It can't. Because for that mother, it could not be worse.

She didn't lose a child in a general or abstract sense. She lost *her* child, and that distinction matters more than people realize. There is no alternate version of that story that makes it easier to live with, no scenario you can point to that softens the reality of what that loss means to her.

It doesn't matter how it happened, how long they lived, or how someone else's story compares. None of those things change the lived experience of losing your child, and none of them make it easier to carry once it has happened.

When someone says, "It could be worse," what often comes through is an attempt to reframe the situation, to suggest that this isn't the worst-case scenario, or that there is something to be grateful for because it didn't happen differently. It's an effort to introduce perspective in a moment that feels overwhelming.

But to a grieving mother, this is the worst-case scenario.

There is no version of this that feels acceptable when you sit with it long enough, and there is no comparison that softens the reality of what has been lost. Grief like this doesn't exist in relation to other people's pain; it exists fully on its own, complete in its impact and impossible to measure against anything else.

And when you try to soften it by comparing it to something worse, it doesn't bring comfort. Just like the phrase "at least," "it could be worse" minimizes the experience, not intentionally, but in a way that reshapes something deeply personal into something that feels smaller and more manageable from the outside.

But it isn't manageable.

There is no perspective that makes it smaller, no comparison that makes it better, and no version of this where losing your child becomes something you can balance against another outcome and feel relieved. At its core, it remains what it is—the worst thing that could happen—and trying to place it within a scale doesn't change that.

Because losing your child is already the worst thing that could happen to you, and no amount of comparison changes that reality.

Grief like this doesn't need perspective. It doesn't need comparison, and it doesn't need to be measured against anyone else's pain. What it needs is to be acknowledged for exactly what it is, without trying to reshape it into something easier to understand.

What you might have meant:

"I'm trying to find a way to make this feel less overwhelming."
"I don't know how to sit with something this painful."
"I wish there were a way to make this easier for you."

What you could have said instead:

"This is devastating."
"I'm so sorry."
"I'm here with you."

You don't need to compare her loss to anything else because to her, there is nothing worse than this.

"This is part of God's plan."

There is a very specific kind of silence that follows loss. It isn't the kind that feels peaceful or restful. It's the kind where the world keeps moving around you, where conversations continue and routines carry on, and you are left standing in it, trying to understand how everything didn't stop with you. There is a disconnect between what has happened inside you and what the world expects you to do next, and that space between the two can feel impossibly wide.

And into that silence, people start talking.

Not because they have the right words, but because they feel like they need to say something, anything, to fill the space. Even when there are no words that can actually ease this kind of pain, the instinct is still to try, and so the words come anyway, often shaped by whatever belief system feels most steady to the person offering them.

"This is part of God's plan."

"God needed another angel."

Before I say anything else, I want to be clear that this is not an attempt to tell anyone what they should or should not believe. For many people, faith is a source of comfort. It provides structure, meaning, and something to hold onto when everything else feels uncertain. I have seen the kind of peace it can bring, and I understand why people reach for it in moments like this.

But what I am talking about here is what it feels like when those words do not land as comfort.

My son was born prematurely. He lived for five minutes. Five minutes where he was here, where I could hold him, where he was mine in a way that felt both complete and impossibly brief. And in the middle of trying to understand how something so significant could exist in such a small amount of time, people tried to give me reasons for it. They told me it was part of a plan. They told me he was needed somewhere else.

What that sounded like, whether it was intended or not, was something very different.

It sounded like this was supposed to happen. That I was meant to carry this. That my son was taken for a reason that mattered more than the fact that he was mine, more than the life he was supposed to have here. It introduced the idea that this loss was not random, not senseless, but intentional in a way that required me to accept it. And I couldn't reconcile that.

If this is part of a plan, then what kind of plan is it? What kind of God, a creator who is supposed to love what He has made, allows this kind of pain? What kind of plan gives my son five minutes with me and leaves me with a lifetime without him? And if God needed another angel, why him? Why *my* child? Why does that need outweigh the life he was supposed to have here?

He wasn't something to be needed somewhere else.

He was mine, and I needed him here. I still do.

Those words didn't bring me closer to faith. I didn't want to walk away, but those words created distance, and I didn't know how to stay without becoming angry. Not surface-level anger, but the kind that settles deeper, the kind that begins to reshape how you see things and what you believe about them.

It felt like my only options were to walk away, or to stay and begin to hate a God I had been raised to believe I was supposed to worship. I didn't want either of those things. I didn't want to lose my faith on top of losing my son, but I also couldn't hold onto it the way it had been given to me.

Because the version of God I had been taught to believe in was one I could no longer reconcile with what I had lived through.

That doesn't mean I believe in nothing. I can't look at my children and believe they came from nothing and will return to nothing. I can't look at the world and feel like there isn't something bigger than us, something beyond what we fully understand. But I also can't believe in God the way He was handed to me—a way that asks me to accept this kind of loss as part of a plan, a way that tells me this pain was intentional, a way that requires me to find peace in something that felt like it broke me.

And this is the part that matters when those words are said to someone else.

When you offer that explanation to a grieving mother, you are not just offering comfort; you are introducing something she now has to carry alongside her grief. If she believes you, then she has to reconcile her loss with the idea that it was meant to happen. If she can't believe you, then she is left questioning something that may have been a foundational part of her life.

Either way, it adds weight.

It creates tension where there was already pain, and it can create distance instead of connection in a moment where connection is what is needed most.

What you might have meant:

"I want to give you something steady when everything feels broken."
"I'm trying to offer comfort in the only way I know how."
"I don't know how to sit in this without trying to make sense of it."

What you could have said instead:

"I'm so sorry."
"I'm here."
"I'll sit with you in this."

If you are reading this as a mother who has lost a child, you don't need a reason. You don't need your grief explained in a way that makes it easier for someone else to hold, and you don't need your child turned into something symbolic so that the loss feels more acceptable from the outside. Sometimes the most compassionate thing someone can do is simply acknowledge that it doesn't make sense, and stay present anyway.

"God doesn't give you more than you can handle."

"God doesn't give you more than you can handle."

This is often said with the intention of reassurance. It's meant to frame pain in a way that feels purposeful, to suggest there is something within you, some level of strength, that matches what you have been given. The message underneath it is meant to comfort, to say that you will survive this because you are capable of surviving it.

But that isn't how it feels.

There is nothing about losing a child that feels manageable. There is nothing about it that fits into the idea of something you were built to handle or prepared to carry. It doesn't arrive in a way that feels proportionate to anything you are or anything you have done, and it certainly doesn't feel like something assigned based on your ability to endure it.

When Jaxon died, I didn't take a breath and think, okay, I can do this. There was no moment of clarity where I felt strong enough or capable enough to carry what had just happened. There was no sense of being equipped for it. There was only the reality that it had happened, and that I was still here, whether I felt ready or not.

Because if God doesn't give you more than you can handle, and this was given to me, then what does that say? It forces a question I couldn't stop asking myself: why me? What made me more capable of handling this than someone else who hasn't experienced this kind of loss? What is it about me that says I was somehow strong enough for this when I didn't feel strong at all?

I didn't feel capable.

No part of me felt prepared for it, and no part of me believed I had the strength people were trying to assign to me. I wasn't standing in it thinking I could handle it; I was standing in it because I didn't have a choice. And there is a difference between those two things that matters more than people realize.

Survival is not the same as strength.

Just because someone is still standing does not mean what they are carrying is bearable. It means they are continuing because there is no alternative, because the world does not stop and offer you the option to step out of your life when something like this happens. You may not be equipped to keep moving, but you do because you have to. When people frame that as strength, it can once again start to feel like pressure.

If this is something I am "strong enough" for, then what does it mean on the days when I fall apart? What does it mean when I can't hold it together, when I feel like I am breaking under the weight of it? Does that mean I am failing at something I was supposed to be able to do?

That isn't comfort. It's expectation, placed on top of something that already feels impossible.

And for someone who has any kind of faith background, there is another layer to that expectation that can be even harder to carry. When you are told that God gave you this because you could handle it, it doesn't just frame your pain—it assigns it. It suggests that this loss was chosen for you, that this level of suffering was intentionally placed in your life because you were capable of enduring it.

And that creates a different kind of question.

If this was given to me, then what does that say about the one who gave it? How do you reconcile the idea of a loving God with the belief that this was something He chose for you? How do you hold onto that without it changing the way you see everything you were taught to believe?

For me, those questions didn't bring comfort.

They created distance.

They made it harder to hold onto something that was supposed to feel like support because instead of carrying me through the pain, it started to feel like the source of it. And that is a complicated place to exist, especially when faith has been something you have relied on your entire life.

Because now it isn't just grief you are trying to navigate. It's everything that grief touches.

It's what you believe, what you were taught, and what still makes sense in the aftermath of something that never will.

And at the center of it all is a truth that doesn't change, no matter how it is framed. It doesn't matter whether I can get through this. I shouldn't have to.

What you might have meant:

"I believe you're strong."
"I hope you find a way through this."
"I don't know how to make this better, but I want to remind you that you're not alone."

What you could have said instead:

"You don't have to be strong right now."
"This is too much, and I'm so sorry."
"I'm here to help carry whatever I can."

You don't need to be told you can handle this. You need people who understand that you shouldn't have to.

Thoughts From Other Mothers

Not every story in this book comes from someone ready to say it out loud.

Some of these voices come from women who are still in it, still close enough to the loss that putting words to it feels impossible, or at least too heavy to carry publicly. The kind of pain that doesn't always translate easily into conversation. It's always there, but saying it makes it real in a way that can feel overwhelming.

Sometimes, silence isn't avoidance. Sometimes it's survival.

There are also women who have shared pieces of their story with me privately, in conversations that were never meant for an audience. Moments of honesty that weren't shaped for a page, but trusted to me in a way that I don't take lightly. And in some of those conversations, I found myself listening differently—not just hearing what was said, but feeling the weight of what wasn't.

This is one of those stories. It comes from someone I love dearly, someone who is still navigating her grief in a way that is deeply personal, someone who chose to remain anonymous but still wanted her experience to be part of this. She trusted me to take what we talked about and shape it into something that reflects what she's living, in a way that feels true to her.

Some stories don't arrive fully formed. Sometimes they are pieced together from conversations, from pauses, from the things someone is able to say and the things they aren't yet ready to.

This is one of them.

Anonymous

I lost my teenage son very recently, in a way no parent should ever have to experience. And now everyone has something to say.

I have people in my life who love me, people who have been there for my family for years, people who are showing up in the ways they know how. I know they mean well, and I know none of what they say is meant to hurt. But some of it does.

Not because they don't care, but because this kind of pain doesn't respond to words the way people hope it will. It isn't something that can be fixed, and it isn't something that fits neatly into the kinds of experiences most people are used to navigating.

I'm not saying other loss isn't real.

I know it is. Losing someone you love changes you. It stays with you. It reshapes your life in ways that don't go away. But this feels different.

Not in a way that compares pain, but in the way it carries its own set of questions, its own set of what-ifs that don't settle, that don't have clean answers. And sometimes, when people try to relate, it doesn't feel like connection.

It creates distance. There's something else I've noticed too. After losing him, people started talking about the signs—what to look for, what should have been noticed, what could have been done differently. I understand why they do that. People want answers. They want to believe there is something they can control, something they can watch for so this never happens to them.

But what about the ones who didn't show any signs?

What about the kids who smiled, who looked okay, who didn't give you anything to point to ahead of time?

Because that matters too.

And sometimes, the way people talk about it feels like blame, even when it isn't meant that way. It can sound like if I had just listened longer, paid closer attention, loved him differently, maybe this wouldn't have happened.

But if my love could have kept him here, if it could have brought him back, he would be immortal.

Then there are the questions.

People ask how it happened. They say they can't imagine. They want details, explanations, something that helps them understand what they're looking at from the outside. But I don't always have those answers.

And even if I did, I don't want to relive it over and over again to provide them. I don't want to explain something that doesn't make sense to me either, and I don't owe anyone a version of my trauma that makes it easier for them to process. Sometimes it's a relief to talk to someone who isn't asking anything.

Someone who lets me exist without needing a response, without trying to guide the conversation somewhere more comfortable.

One of the hardest moments was when someone tried to comfort me by telling me what a great kid he was, and then followed it with, "He just made a bad choice," repeating it like that was the explanation that would make it easier to accept.

All I could think was: don't reduce him to that.

Don't take everything he was and shrink it down to one moment, one decision, one version of his life that ignores everything else. He was funny, he was talented, he was caring, and he was mine.

That's what I wish people understood.

This kind of loss doesn't need to be explained, and it doesn't need to be analyzed in a way that tries to make sense of something that doesn't. It just needs to be felt, in whatever way it shows up, without someone trying to reshape it into something easier to look at from the outside.

Chapter Six
Cruelty

The Life I Thought I'd Have

Grief has layers.

Every loss does, but losing a child creates a kind of layered grief that people don't always recognize because not all of it is visible. There is the grief of losing your child, which is the part people understand most easily. It's tangible in a way they can point to, something they can name and acknowledge as a clear absence.

There is also the grief of the person you were before. That version of you, the one who existed before loss reshaped everything, feels more abstract, but people can still see it. They notice that something in you has changed, that there is a difference in how you move through the world, even if they can't fully explain it. Just like with secondary losses.

But then there is another layer, one that is much harder for people to grasp. You grieve the life you thought you were going to have.

That loss is invisible. It's as real as any other layer, but it never had the chance to become something others could see. There are no pictures to look back on, no memories to revisit, no milestones that can be named or shared. There is no physical proof that it ever existed outside of you.

There are only expectations.

Hopes.

Plans that felt solid at the time, a future that felt real enough to imagine in detail, until the moment it wasn't there anymore. And that kind of grief is quiet.

It lives in the space of what should have been, in the moments that pass where you suddenly realize what is missing. It shows up in ordinary experiences that take on a different meaning, when you catch yourself thinking about where they would have been, what you would have been doing, who they might have become if things had gone differently.

It appears in the absence of things that never happen. A birthday that never gets celebrated. A first day of school that never comes. Conversations you never get to have.

And because those moments never existed outside of you, people don't always understand why they hurt. From the outside, it can look like you are grieving something that wasn't real. And when you try to put it into words, it can sometimes sound like you are unhappy with the life you have now, or that you are overlooking what is still present in front of you.

But that isn't what this is. You can love the life you have and still grieve the one you lost. Those two things don't cancel each other out, and they don't compete for space. They exist alongside each other, shaping the way you experience your life in ways that are difficult to explain but are very real.

Grief is not only about what was. It is also about what should have been. And learning to live with that means carrying both at the same time—the life you have, and the life you thought you were going to have.

The Part I Almost Didn't Write

Full disclosure: I wrote the entire book before I wrote this section.

I didn't want to write it, even though it matters. It is easier to talk about general experiences, about the patterns in what people say, and about the ways grief is misunderstood than it is to sit in the moments that changed your life in ways that can't be undone. But this book is meant to help people understand what this kind of loss actually does to you, and I can't do that honestly if I avoid the parts that were the hardest to live through.

So this is my experience.

I'm not going to speak for my husband because I can't. I don't know what this loss felt like from his side in the same way I know it from mine, and I've been very intentional about not trying to fill in those gaps. As our four-year-old recently explained while learning about boys and girls, "Mommy doesn't have a neener. She's a girl." And while that is apparently the most important distinction in our house right now, the point still stands: our experiences are not the same.

What I can tell you is what was said—and what it did.

"Maybe this is God's way of telling you that you shouldn't be together."

That was said to him. And while he didn't listen, I did.

I heard it, and for a time, I believed it, because grief has a way of breaking down the parts of you that would normally reject something like that. It doesn't just leave you sad; it leaves you vulnerable and makes room for thoughts that don't belong to you to settle in anyway. That statement didn't feel like someone else's opinion. It felt like confirmation of something I was already afraid might be true—that I was a failure, that he deserved better, and that losing our son was somehow proof that we were never supposed to exist together in the first place.

And once that idea takes hold, it doesn't stay contained.

It shows up in quiet moments, in the spaces where you are already struggling to hold yourself together, and it starts to reshape how you see yourself. It fed into something heavier for me, something I don't say lightly and don't say often: the thought that everything might be easier if I simply wasn't here at all. I didn't want to end my life, but the weight of everything felt impossible to carry. And that statement gave that feeling somewhere to land.

But here is the part that matters.

He stayed.

Not because it was easy, not because everything around us was supportive or encouraging, and not because anyone made space for us to grieve together in a way that brought us closer. He stayed because he chose to. He chose me, and he chose us, in a moment where it would have been easier to let doubt take over, easier to listen to the noise around us, easier to walk away from something that had just been broken in a way neither of us knew how to fix.

He didn't.

And that choice mattered more than anything that was said.

Because while those words were planting doubt in me, they weren't shaping him in the same way. While I was questioning my worth and my place in his life, he was still standing in it, still showing up, still choosing to build something with me even when everything around us felt unstable. And over time, that choice became something stronger than the doubt that had been handed to us.

We grew up very differently. My family was complicated, and connection was not something that came easily or consistently. His was close-knit, the kind of family people picture when they talk about support systems. I would love to say that losing our son brought us all together, that something that significant created understanding and softened the way people showed up for us.

But that isn't what happened.

And I want to be clear about something, because this part matters too.

It wasn't everyone.

There were people who showed up for us in ways that mattered, people who made space for us, who loved us without hesitation and without conditions. **Shoutout Grandma D—she**

supported us from the very beginning and always made me feel welcome, like I belonged. That kind of presence doesn't go unnoticed, and it doesn't get forgotten.

But the damage done elsewhere still mattered.

I won't go into every detail of the last seventeen years because that could be its own book, but I will say this: that moment mattered more than I think anyone who said it understood. It didn't just minimize our loss—it gave it a direction. It suggested that something so devastating had a purpose beyond grief, one that created distance instead of connection and reinforced the idea that I didn't belong.

And that feeling didn't stay in that moment.

It shaped what came after.

For a long time, I tried to bridge that gap. I showed up, I made the effort, I sat in rooms where I knew I wasn't fully welcome, and I chose to stay quiet about things that should have been addressed. I celebrated people who didn't celebrate us and ignored what I knew was being said behind our backs, not because it was deserved, but because I loved my husband and didn't want to be the reason he felt pushed outside of something that mattered to him.

I tried to create connection where there wasn't one.

And eventually, I realized I didn't have to.

Because the life we built together didn't depend on their acceptance.

Our family is real, complete, and deeply loved. It includes every child we have brought into this world and every child we have carried in ways others can't always see. It is full in a way that doesn't need validation from anyone outside of it. And once I understood that, the need to keep reaching for something that was never fully there started to fade.

That doesn't mean everything disappeared.

There is still a relationship, but it exists on the surface. It is polite, it is distant, and it requires effort on our part to maintain. We are not part of that inner circle, and over time I have come to understand that this is not just because of how they feel about me, but because I no longer want to force my way into a space that never made room for us to begin with.

What I do have is my husband.

He is my best friend. He chose me in the middle of grief, in the middle of doubt, in the middle of everything that could have pulled us apart, and we built something stronger because of it. The love we have now is not dependent on anyone else's approval, and it doesn't need to be.

But there is a reality that hasn't changed.

They didn't make space for my son.

And seventeen years later, that has shaped the way they experience our children now. Children notice more than we give them credit for. They see who shows up, they feel who chooses them, and they move toward the people who make them feel loved and accepted without hesitation.

And the truth is, the people who chose not to fully step into our family are missing out on something extraordinary.

So if there is a point to all of this, it is this:

Words hold weight.

A lot of this book is about things said with good intentions, but this is what happens when the intention isn't good, or when it is careless enough that it might as well not be. Words like that don't disappear. They shape relationships, they change how you see people, and they stay with you long after the moment has passed.

No amount of time erases how someone treated you in your darkest moment. So if you ever have the opportunity to speak into someone's grief, even if you don't like them, choose to love them through it, because the alternative doesn't just hurt in the moment. It changes everything that comes after.

"Why do you keep trying?"

"Why do you keep trying?"

That question was followed by something even harder to hear.

"Why do you keep having babies knowing they will probably just die?"

That wasn't said by a stranger or someone distant enough to dismiss. It came from my sister—someone who was supposed to know me and love me in a way that made space for both my grief and my choices. And that is what made it land the way it did.

By the time those words were said, Jaxon wasn't my first loss. I had already lived through multiple pregnancies that didn't end the way they were supposed to. I had a condition that caused early labor, and loss was not something new or unexpected in my story. It was already something I was carrying, trying to navigate without fully understanding how.

But in that moment, none of that mattered in the way it should have. Instead of being seen as loss, it was reduced to a pattern. Something that should have been recognized, something that should have been stopped, something that could have been avoided if I had made different choices. And just like that, what I had experienced wasn't treated as grief. It was treated as something preventable, something I had continued despite knowing the risk. As if the solution to losing children was to stop trying to have them.

There is a particular kind of pain that comes from having your love reframed as a mistake. Because that is what those words did. They didn't just question my decisions; they questioned the validity of my hope, my desire to be a mother, and my willingness to continue loving even when that love came with risk. They suggested that the answer was to let fear dictate my future, to let loss define what I was allowed to want going forward.

But love doesn't work like that.

Hope doesn't shut off just because it has been broken before. The desire to be a mother doesn't disappear simply because it has come with pain. Those things don't operate on logic or caution, and they don't disappear just because someone else thinks they should.

What she was really saying, whether she realized it or not, was that I should let my pain decide my future, that I should allow fear to become the thing that shapes what I do next. And I didn't.

I look at the children I had after, the ones I carried and delivered early, the ones we brought into our family through adoption, and I cannot imagine my life without them. Not for a second. Not for a safer version of my life, and not for a version where I avoided more loss.

Because avoiding pain would have meant losing them too. And that is not a trade I would ever make. But that doesn't mean those words didn't change something. They did.

Some things don't only hurt in the moment—they alter how you see the person who said them. They shift something fundamental in the relationship, something that doesn't easily return to what it was before, no matter how much time passes.

That relationship didn't recover.

We went from being family to being nothing, not because I wanted that outcome, but because there are things you don't come back from once they have been said out loud. There are moments that draw a line so clearly that you can't pretend it isn't there, even if you wish you could.

Maybe she didn't understand the weight of what she said. But I felt it—every single part of it. And I carried it long after the moment was over.

Loving my children, even knowing the risks, was never the wrong choice.

What you might have meant:

"I'm scared for you."
"I don't want to see you hurt again."
"I don't understand how you keep going."

What you could have said instead:

"I'm here for you, no matter what you choose."
"I trust you to make the right decision for your family."
"I love you."

Grief doesn't get to decide whether we love again, and fear doesn't get to decide whether we try again. Loss does not take away our capacity to be mothers, and it does not mean we have no more love to give.

"Silver linings."

"Try to find the silver lining."

"Stop being so gloomy."

"There has to be something good that comes from this."

This is one of those phrases that tends to show up as time goes on, usually after the initial shock has passed and people begin to feel like grief should start changing into something more manageable. There is an unspoken expectation behind it, a sense that at some point you are supposed to take something this devastating and turn it into something positive, something meaningful, something easier for other people to sit with.

I have never understood that expectation.

The idea of finding a "silver lining" suggests that there is something within the loss itself that can be reframed into good, something that balances what was taken. But silver is a shade of gray, and even in that metaphor, it is still part of the storm. The thing you are asking me to find something good in is the same thing that completely unraveled my life, and there is no version of that where it suddenly becomes something worth appreciating if I just look at it from the right angle.

And the "silver linings" people offer are rarely neutral.

They tend to come in the form of explanations meant to assign value to the loss, statements that try to reshape it into something productive. One of the most common versions I have heard is the idea that I am a better mother to my other children because of what I went through.

…Tha fuck?

How can you possibly know that? How can you take something I never got the chance to experience and decide that the version of me before loss would have been less capable, less present, less loving? That isn't something you can measure, and it isn't something you get to define.

And even if I am different now, even if grief has changed the way I parent, that change did not come from something beautiful. It came from something that broke me. It came from loss, from fear, from a kind of awareness I never wanted to have in the first place.

People have a tendency to look for meaning in pain because it makes it easier to accept. If something good can be pulled from it, then it feels less senseless, less random, less cruel. It gives the illusion that there is balance and that something can be gained to offset what was taken.

Not everything needs to be turned into a lesson. It doesn't need a positive spin to justify its existence. The beauty people are trying to point to doesn't exist within the loss itself. It exists in what comes after, in the way you rebuild, in the way you continue, in the way you find moments of love and connection again despite what has happened, not because of it.

I am the mother I am today in spite of losing him, not because of it.

Grief is not a gift.

Loss is not a blessing.

And you do not have to find something good in something that was never okay.

What you might have meant:

"I'm trying to find something that makes this feel less painful."
"I want to believe something good can come from something so terrible."
"I don't know how to sit with something that doesn't have a positive side."

What you could have said instead:

"This is unfair."
"This shouldn't have happened."
"I'm so sorry."

You don't have to find a silver lining. Sometimes things are just dark, and pretending otherwise doesn't make them easier to carry. Sometimes the most honest thing you can do is acknowledge that something was devastating and allow it to be exactly that, without trying to reshape it into something more acceptable.

Losing him didn't make me less of a mother. If anything, it changed the way I understand what being a mother actually means. It deepened it in ways I never expected and never would have chosen but that are real all the same. Motherhood, for me, is not defined only by the children I get to raise in front of the world. It includes the child I carry with me in ways that are less visible but no less significant.

I still carry him with me. He exists in the way I think, in the way I move through the world, in the way I love the children who are here. He is present in the awareness I have of how fragile life is, in the way I hold onto moments a little tighter, and in the way I see things other people might not notice. He is part of me, not as something separate or distant, but as something woven into who I have become.

Even if the world doesn't see him, I do. And that matters. His life, no matter how brief, shaped mine, and that doesn't disappear just because it isn't visible to anyone else. He is still part of my story, still part of my family, still part of the way I understand love and loss and everything that exists in between.

And I have learned that I don't need the world to recognize that for it to be true.

Thoughts From Other Mothers

Not every loss looks the same, but the way people respond to it often follows the same patterns.

One of the things I've learned while writing this book is how many different forms loss can take, and how often those experiences are misunderstood in similar ways. The words may change slightly, the circumstances may be different, but the impact of what is said—and what is left unsaid—can feel strikingly familiar.

Brianna is one of those voices.

Her losses included multiple miscarriages and a failed IVF cycle, and like so many women, she was met with comments that tried to reframe her pain into something more acceptable, something easier for other people to understand.

This is her perspective.

Brianna S.

Well, the guy I was trying to have a baby with and I are no longer together, so people will say that it's a good thing that I had those miscarriages. I had three and a failed IVF. That statement did not help. I still want my babies. Also, something that would have helped would have been if more people actually cared. It felt like I went through them alone.

Some people would tell me that they were sorry about what I was going through, but unless you've experienced it, you don't realize how extremely depressing it is. Which I actually get because I also did not realize and actually apologized to a couple of my friends who had had them previously, before I ever experienced it, and I apologized to them for not being there more for them.

So now if someone close to me experiences something like this, I get them a small tree to plant, typically a cherry blossom. That way, they can watch it grow as the baby would have grown. I just wish that more people understood how heartbreaking it is.

Chapter Seven
As Time Goes On

The Version of Me that Stayed Behind

THERE'S A VERSION OF ME THAT still exists in a time before all of this.

I don't visit her often, but sometimes I catch a glimpse of her in old photos, in memories that feel lighter, or in those rare moments when I almost recognize the person I used to be. She feels familiar but distant, like someone I knew intimately once and can still remember clearly, even though I can't get back to her. She didn't know.

She didn't know how fragile everything was or how quickly life could change. She didn't know what it felt like to carry something like this, to live in the aftermath of a loss that doesn't just hurt you, but rearranges you. There are parts of her I miss more than I know how to explain. I miss the way life felt simpler then, the way happiness didn't seem to come with an edge to it, and the way the world didn't feel like it could split open at any moment and take everything with it.

And if I could go back, I would.

I would go back even knowing exactly how it ends, even knowing I couldn't change a single thing. I would relive it. I would walk straight into that pain again, a thousand times over, if it meant I got those five minutes with him one more time. That's the part people may not understand from the outside. This grief is unbearable, yes, but it is still attached to him. And when the choice is between never having had him at all or living through the pain of losing him again, I would choose him. Every time.

So that version of me stayed there, and I kept going.

Not as someone stronger, and not as someone better, but as someone different. Loss changed the way I move through the world. It made me more aware, more careful, and more conscious of how quickly everything can change. There is a weight I carry now that I didn't before. It isn't always crushing, and it doesn't always announce itself loudly, but it is always there. It shows up in the way I love, in the way I hold onto moments a little tighter, and in the way I look at my children with the constant awareness of how much can be lost.

Losing him didn't take everything from me, but it changed everything *about* me. And I have learned to live with that, not by forgetting who I used to be, but by accepting that she no longer exists in the same way. Neither does the version of my life where he does. That is part of what grief asks you to carry—not just the child you lost, but the self who existed before that loss, and the future that disappeared with it.

So I carry both.

The life I have, and the life I lost.

Not as something I am trying to fix, but as something that simply is.

Watching Them Grow

There are moments that catch you off guard, not because they are big or overwhelming, but because they are so completely ordinary. A birthday party, a school event, or a random afternoon where everything feels normal can suddenly shift you in a way no one else notices.

It happens quietly. You see a child the age he would have been, and there is a brief realization that settles in before you can stop it. He should be here too. Nothing in the room changes. Conversations continue, people laugh, life moves forward exactly as it should, but inside, something shifts just enough to remind you of what is missing.

I find myself doing the math sometimes, even now.

I think about how old he would be and how his life might have fit into the one we are living. His sisters are teenagers, and I can picture him in those moments with them, driving them and their friends around, laughing, rolling his eyes, pretending to be annoyed while secretly loving it. I wonder what kind of relationship they would have had, whether they would share the kind of inside jokes that only siblings understand.

His little brothers are still so small, and I imagine that version of him too. I think about whether he would wrestle with them on the floor, letting them win just enough to keep them trying, but not enough to make it obvious. I think about whether he would beat them at video games and act like it wasn't even close, the way older siblings do.

These thoughts don't come all at once. They show up in pieces, in the middle of good moments, the kind you want to stay fully present in. Because every memory we make now is also a reminder of one we don't get to have with him.

He would be driving now. He would be getting ready to finish high school. And I find myself wondering what kind of person he would have become. Maybe he would love cooking with me, or maybe he would play guitar with his dad. Maybe he would be an artist, or a scientist, or something I would have never expected at all.

And that's the part that stays with me. These aren't just possibilities I'm imagining for fun. They are pieces of a life that never got the chance to unfold, questions that will never have answers no matter how much time passes. There is no version of the future where I get to know those things, no moment where those unknowns resolve into something real.

And the world doesn't stop for that either.

These kids keep growing. They hit milestones, they become more of who they are meant to be, and I get to witness all of it. I am happy for that. I truly am. But there is always something sitting just underneath it.

It doesn't take away from the joy but exists alongside it—a quiet ache that doesn't ask for attention, but never fully leaves. It isn't about not being happy for them.

It's about him.

It's about everything I don't get to witness, everything I don't get to experience, and everything I don't get to know. There is no closure in that, just questions that don't have answers and moments that come and go without warning.

I've learned not to fight those thoughts. They're not there to hurt me. They're there because he mattered, because he still does, and because love doesn't disappear just because the person you love isn't physically here. And maybe I don't get to watch him grow. But I carry the version of him that only I will ever know.

"This isn't normal."

"This isn't healthy."

"This isn't normal."

There is something deeply unsettling about being told how you should be grieving by people who have never experienced this kind of loss. It takes something that is already difficult to navigate and turns it into something that feels observed and evaluated, as if grief is supposed to follow a recognizable pattern that can be measured from the outside.

It often comes with an unspoken expectation—that this is temporary, that this level of pain should eventually settle into something quieter, something easier to witness. It's treated like a phase, like a bad stretch of time that should pass if handled correctly, as though losing a child is something that can be processed, resolved, and eventually placed somewhere manageable.

But there is nothing about this that fits into anything I would ever call normal. So why would be grief be expected to?

Grief like this doesn't move in a straight line, and it doesn't present itself in ways that are easy to recognize or categorize. It is layered, unpredictable, and often contradictory because the loss itself is all those things. When something happens that disrupts your life at that level, your response to it is not going to look polished or controlled. It is going to be messy. It is going to be overwhelming. And at times, it is going to show up in ways that don't make sense to anyone but you.

And when people describe that as "not healthy," what they are often responding to is their own discomfort. What would actually be unhealthy is pretending it didn't happen, pushing it down, or trying to reshape it into something more acceptable so it becomes easier for others to sit with. Ignoring grief doesn't remove it. It forces it to find its way out later, often in ways that are harder to manage and harder to understand.

Allowing yourself to feel it, as painful as that is, is not a sign that something is wrong. It is part of surviving it.

That doesn't mean it has to look a certain way, and it doesn't mean it will always be visible. It simply means you are allowing the reality of what happened to exist, instead of trying to force it into a version that makes other people more comfortable.

People tend to label grief when it challenges their idea of what is acceptable. If it lasts longer than they expect, it becomes "unhealthy." If it shows up in ways they don't know how to respond to, it becomes "not normal." But those labels don't come from an understanding of grief. They come from an inability to sit with something that doesn't have a clear shape or an easy resolution.

And grief is not comfortable to witness. It is about survival. And surviving something like this is not going to look normal because there is nothing normal about what you are trying to live through.

What you might have meant:

"I'm worried about you."
"I don't understand this, and it scares me."
"I want you to be okay, and I don't know what that looks like."

What you could have said instead:

"I'm here for you."
"You don't have to hide how you're feeling."
"I'm not going anywhere."

Grief doesn't need to look normal to be valid, and it doesn't need to look healthy to be necessary. Sometimes, the only way to survive something like this is to feel it exactly as it is.

"It's time to move on."

"It's been a while now…"

"Don't you think it's time to move on?"

"You can't stay stuck forever."

These are the kinds of statements that tend to come later, after enough time has passed that people begin to feel like grief should have softened into something less visible. There is an assumption behind them, one that suggests there is a natural endpoint to pain, a place where it becomes quiet enough that it no longer needs to be acknowledged in the same way.

But grief doesn't work like that.

There is no invisible clock counting down to the moment where losing a child becomes something you can neatly place behind you. There is no day when you wake up and feel like enough time has passed for it to make sense, or for it to hurt in a way that feels acceptable to others.

Time does change things, but not in the way people often expect. It creates distance between the moments that feel unbearable, and it allows you to function in ways that may not have been possible in the beginning. It makes space for laughter to return, for routines to rebuild, and for life to continue in ways that can look, from the outside, like healing. But beneath all of that, the loss itself remains unchanged. It doesn't shrink, and it doesn't resolve into something easier to carry simply because more time has passed.

What changes is how you live with it. And that is where the misunderstanding often happens.

When people talk about "moving on," what they are usually imagining is a version of life where the loss becomes distant, where it fades into the background and no longer shapes the present in a meaningful way. It sounds like closure, like something that can be completed, something that belongs to the past instead of continuing to exist in the present.

But losing a child does not fit into that kind of ending.

You don't move on from your child, because there is no version of that where they stop being yours. Instead, you move forward with their memory, carrying the love that never went away and learning how to exist alongside the absence that never fully does either. They are still part of your life, not in the way you imagined, but in a way that is constant and real, even if it is not always visible to anyone else.

So when someone says it's time to move on, what it can feel like is an expectation to let go of something that was never meant to be temporary. It can sound like you have grieved long enough, like the depth of what you feel should have lessened by now, or like the continued presence of that grief is somehow a sign that you are not moving forward in the way you should be.

But this isn't something you let go of.

Because letting go of the grief would mean letting go of the connection, and that connection is all that remains of a relationship that never ended in the way it was supposed to. Grief does not exist because someone is stuck. It exists because someone was loved deeply, and that kind of love does not disappear just because time has passed. It becomes part of how you move through the world.

That doesn't mean life stops or that joy isn't possible. Life does continue. There is laughter again, there are moments that feel full and meaningful, and there are days where the weight of everything feels lighter than it once did. But those moments do not replace the grief, and they do not cancel it out. They exist alongside it, shaped by the quiet understanding that someone is missing from all of it.

And learning to carry that does not mean you are stuck. It means you have adapted to something you never should have had to carry in the first place.

Grief doesn't follow a timeline, and it doesn't end in a way that fits into other people's expectations. It changes shape, it becomes something you learn to carry, and it settles into your life in ways that are quieter but no less real. And the most compassionate thing you can do is not expect someone to move on, but to stay with them as they learn how to keep going.

What you might have meant:

"I don't want you to stay in pain forever."
"I want to see you living your life again."
"I'm hoping things feel a little lighter for you now."

What you could have said instead:

"I'm still here for you, no matter how much time has passed."
"You don't have to rush this."
"I'm here, always."

Thoughts From Other Mothers

Not all of the voices in this book come from people I know personally.

Some of them come from moments where I was simply honest about what I was writing and invited others to share their experiences if they wanted to. Tabitha is one of those voices. She responded to a post I made about this book, and her words stayed with me.

There is a weight to what she shared, something that doesn't need to be softened or reinterpreted to be understood. It stands on its own in a way that feels both deeply personal and painfully familiar. Her words deserve to be heard.

Tabitha L.

I struggle so often with what to share and what not to share with others. I genuinely feel like people need to learn how to navigate death, grief, depression, etc. People are not as supportive as they think they are. People say things, and I believe they genuinely think they are helping—but the truth is, it is not helpful at all. Sometimes people come off as rude or inconsiderate.

All I know is people need to shift from grief as a problem to be solved to an experience needing support.

You "know" I'm struggling but you don't know how much and you never will. People always offer to lend an ear, but the truth is, if they knew exactly how much pain was harbored, how the thoughts never stop, they wouldn't offer. They'd grow bored and tired of listening. They'd give the same blanket response as anyone else: "it's time to move on" or "stop being so negative."

When I finally open up and speak of my son and people try to change the subject, they might think they're being helpful—maybe trying to "take my mind off it"? It's not helpful. It's painful. It makes me feel dismissed. It makes me feel like my son is chucked aside and ignored as well.

People often wince at the sound of my son's name rolling off my tongue, and they're equally hesitant to say his name around me. I notice it every time. It is heartbreaking. A mother who has lost her son doesn't want others to stop speaking of him.

She wants you to say his name.

Out loud.

Saying his name is the only way to keep his memory alive.

Braeden.

His name is Braeden.

"It's been ___ years."

"At least you got almost 15 years with him."

"You're not the only one who lost him."

"He's in a better place."

"He wouldn't want you to cry."

"I don't know how you do it."

"You're so strong."

I know it's intended to be, but none of this is helpful or positive.

And I cannot handle the "change your mindset, change your diet, change your life" comments. Sure, those things can help physically, but they have absolutely nothing to do with the toll grief takes on someone's mental and physical health—straight to their core, deep into their soul.

I can eat more, eat less, cut out soda or sugar, change caffeine, or whatever the fuck else someone suggests, but that will never take the pain of losing my son away.

I'm tired of people trying to make it seem like it isn't the most profound, fucked up thing I've ever experienced in my life.

When someone says they don't want to be a burden, this is what they mean. This is why they only share bits and pieces. This is why they say they're okay or give short answers, because the truth is no one actually wants to hear the deepest truths in their rawest form. Not even the people who claim to be the closest to you.

Grief for everyone is different. Some people are motivated by the gym, music, or getting outside. Some need rest. Some need self-care. Some need to be left alone without being judged.

For me, I need all of that in small doses.

Some days I want to get things done and take on the world. Other days I need to curl up in my bed and sit in my feelings for a moment without being pulled out of it by everyday questions.

Not because those things don't matter—but because sometimes I need a moment where I don't have to hold everything together.

I try really hard not to let those moments happen too often. I bury it more than anyone realizes. But when it surfaces, when I can't push it off any further, the feelings need to be felt. And I need to be allowed to feel them without feeling like I'm being judged.

Chapter Eight Reshaping Myself

The First Time I Felt Okay

THERE WAS A MOMENT. I don't remember exactly when it happened, but I remember how it felt.

I laughed, and it wasn't forced or polite or expected of me. It was real. The kind of laugh that comes naturally before you have time to think about it, the kind that feels normal for just a second. And in that moment, I forgot—not him, never him—but the weight of everything that came with losing him. As quickly as it came, it was replaced by something else.

Guilt.

It settled in almost immediately, like I had crossed a line I didn't know existed. There was this feeling that I wasn't supposed to be okay, that if I could laugh like that, even for a second, it meant I wasn't grieving the way I was supposed to. Part of me knew that didn't make sense, but grief doesn't follow logic, and it doesn't care what you understand intellectually. It pulls you into a space where even the smallest moments of relief feel confusing.

After loss, life doesn't come back all at once. It returns in pieces, in moments that almost go unnoticed at first—a conversation that feels normal, a day that isn't quite as heavy, a laugh that catches you off guard. And instead of relief, those moments can feel disorienting, because they come with questions you weren't prepared to answer.

You start wondering what it means.

Whether feeling okay is a sign that you're moving on, or worse, that you're leaving them behind. Whether you're becoming someone less connected to them, someone who is slowly letting go without meaning to. That fear sits under the surface, even when you know, deep down, that it isn't true.

Because it isn't.

Feeling okay doesn't mean he matters less, and it doesn't mean the loss has become smaller or easier to carry. It doesn't mean the love is fading. It means you are still here, still living, still finding your way through something you never chose.

I still have those moments. There are times where I laugh, where I feel happy, where life feels full again in a way I wasn't sure it ever would. And underneath all of it, he is still there, steady and constant in a way that doesn't need to announce itself to be real.

Grief doesn't disappear. It changes shape, and learning how to live with that isn't betrayal—it's survival.

I remember the first year his birthday didn't bring me to my knees in the way it had before. We still talked about him, we still said his name, and he was still very much part of that day, but I didn't have to shut everything down just to get through it. I wasn't undone in the same way, and that realization hit me harder than I expected. Because that pain had started to feel like something I needed.

It felt like proof of how much he mattered, how deeply he was loved, and how significant his absence still was. When it didn't feel as sharp, there was part of me that panicked. If the pain changed, even slightly, it made me question what that meant. If it doesn't hurt the same way, is he farther away from me than he used to be?

To this day, his birthday is the day I let the sadness in without trying to manage it. It's my "okay to not be okay" day, even though realistically it's never just one day. It stretches into the days around it, into the spaces before and after, but that one day carries more weight because I allow it to.

And the first time it didn't hit me as hard as I expected, it stopped me completely.

I know that isn't rational, but grief rarely is. Because when the pain shifts, even a little, it can feel like something important is changing without your permission. And when that pain is one of the only tangible connections you feel like you still have, the idea of it softening can be as unsettling as when it was overwhelming.

"If you need anything, call."

"If you need anything, call."

This is one I didn't fully understand at first.

It sounds kind. It sounds supportive. It feels like the right thing to say when you don't know what else to say, and if I'm being honest, it's something I've said myself more than once without thinking about it.

It wasn't until I started having conversations with other mothers, until I really listened to how this phrase lands on the receiving end, that I realized how much it can actually hurt. What sounds like an offer of support often feels like something else entirely. It puts the responsibility back on her.

Now she has to figure out what she needs, which is not always clear when you're grieving something this overwhelming. She has to sort through the fog, identify what might actually help, build up the energy to ask for it, and risk of being told no or feeling like she asked for too much. That requires a level of clarity and energy that grief does not leave room for.

Grieving a child is not the time for her to manage the people around her. It's not her job to organize support, delegate tasks, or make it easier for others to show up in a way that feels helpful. Most days, she is just trying to get through the next hour without falling apart, and adding another layer of responsibility to that, even one that sounds supportive, can feel like too much.

What many people don't realize is that grief can make even simple decisions feel overwhelming. Choosing what to eat, deciding whether to answer a message, or figuring out how to get through the day can already feel like more than she has the capacity for. So being asked to define what she needs and communicating it clearly doesn't feel like help—it feels like another thing she has to carry.

There is also something else that comes with that phrase.

When someone says, "If you need anything, call," it can feel open-ended in a way that isn't always real. And when a grieving mother finally gathers the strength to reach out and say, "I could really use this," and the response is hesitation or an inability to follow through, it doesn't only feel disappointing, but it reinforces the idea that she asked for too much.

That the support had limits. That "anything" didn't actually mean anything. And it's a moment sticks. She doesn't need more words.

She needs to feel like someone is willing to step into the space with her without being asked. Instead of asking, "What do you need?" it helps to shift into something more concrete. Tell her what you're going to do, and then follow through. Bring dinner. Take care of the other kids for a few hours. Do the dishes without asking where everything goes.

Sit with her in silence without trying to fix anything or fill the space with words.

Those things don't require her to think, decide, or ask. They just happen, and that's what makes them feel supported instead of something she has to manage.

And if you do say, "If you need anything, call," mean it in a way that holds weight. Mean it in a way that leaves room for her to actually reach out without questioning whether she should. Because too often, that phrase is said to fill silence, to offer something without having to define it, and it ends up feeling empty when it matters most.

Support isn't about offering help in a way that feels right to say. It's about showing up in a way that removes something from her plate instead of adding to it.

What you might have meant:

"I care about you, and I don't know what to do, but I want to help."
"I don't want to overstep or do the wrong thing."
"I'm here, I just don't know how to show up."

What you could have said instead:

"I'm bringing dinner over tonight."
"I'll take care of the kids for a few hours this weekend."
"I'm coming by to help clean—no need to host me."
"I'm here. We can sit together, even if we don't say anything."

And if you truly don't know what to do, show up anyway. Presence will always matter more than perfectly chosen words.

"What doesn't kill you makes you stronger."

"What doesn't kill you makes you stronger."

This is one of those phrases that tends to show up after some time has passed, once people decide you've made it through the worst of it and are now standing on the other side in some improved, more resilient form. It's usually said as a compliment, like they're acknowledging something admirable about the way you've handled everything. But that's not how it feels.

In a lot of ways, it *did* kill me—just not in a literal sense. The version of me that existed before loss didn't survive, and that's the part people don't see when they look at me now. They see someone functioning, someone who can laugh, show up, hold conversations, and move through life in a way that looks steady enough to pass for "okay." And from that, they assume I came out stronger, like this was some kind of test I completed and passed.

Like I should be proud of it.

Like I earned something.

Do I get a medal? A certificate? A commemorative mug that says "Survived the Worst Thing Imaginable and All I Got Was This Personality Shift"?

Because that's what it feels like sometimes—like people are applauding something I never volunteered for.

This didn't make me stronger. It made me different. It made me more aware of how fragile everything is, more cautious about what I allow myself to hold onto, and more familiar with a kind of pain I wish I had never learned how to carry. It changed the way I move through the world, the way I think, and the way I protect myself, and none of that came from some empowering transformation. It came from loss.

And yes, it made me funnier.

Objectively.

Like… I'm hilarious now.

But not in a "wow, she's thriving" kind of way. It's more of a "if I don't laugh, I will absolutely spiral into the void and never return" kind of humor. Dark humor isn't a personality upgrade—it's a coping mechanism with better timing. It's how I create just enough space between me and something that could otherwise swallow me whole.

So no, this didn't make me stronger. It made me resourceful. It made me adaptive.

It made me really good at functioning in a world that I now understand can take everything from me without warning and then keep moving like nothing happened. It also made me build walls in places I didn't even know I needed them, not because I want to shut people out, but because I learned the hard way how much can be taken and how quickly it can happen.

When people say, "What doesn't kill you makes you stronger," what I hear is an attempt to give purpose to something that doesn't have one. It's a way of making pain feel more acceptable, more structured, more worth it.

But not everything that hurts has a purpose. And not everything you survive turns you into something better.

Sometimes it just changes you, and you spend the rest of your life figuring out how to exist as someone you never expected to become.

What you might have meant:

"I see how hard this has been, and I admire that you're still going."
"I don't know how you're doing this, but I respect it."
"I'm trying to acknowledge what you've been through."

What you could have said instead:

"You didn't deserve this."
"I'm here for you."
"You don't have to be strong."

Strength isn't something I gained from this. It's something people assigned to me so the pain would make more sense to them, even if it never made sense to me.

Thoughts From Other Mothers

Elissa isn't someone I met through shared loss at first.

She was my neighbor. Her kids were the reason we connected, and I'm pretty sure they decided we were friends before either of us had a say in it. What started as proximity turned into something more, into the kind of connection that grows over time until you realize how much someone has become part of your life.

Her perspective is one that stays with me.

Elissa A.

I think for me, I understood our circle of friends were there for us, but the constant checking in was painful. Most days it was all-consuming, so the brief moments I felt good enough to be on my phone, the waves of grief would hit harder and harder because all that was on my phone were texts asking what I needed and if we were okay. Like, no. I'm not. But thanks.

What we appreciated most were the one-off comments like: "I'm here to listen if/when you're ready to talk about it," or "If you'd like to share how everything happened or share your experience, I can be a listening ear." We received prayer cards specific to losing a child about four months after we lost our son, and it was such perfect timing. I was in a spot mentally to read them, cry, and feel the love of our friends who chose them for us. The lasting positive memories we have are the silent hugs, the small gesture of keeping him in our count of children, recognizing he existed even if we don't get to watch him grow, only having a memory of him.

Lastly, the way our circle let the kids talk about him in every way they needed to in order to process what happened. Letting them grieve the loss of a little brother that they got to feel through my belly but never got to meet was a special circumstance that I'm not sure everyone can wrap their head around. so watching our kids process in their own way with such supportive adults was the biggest gift of all. It was a true "it takes a village" season that could have turned out so much worse if we didn't have those experiences with friends, neighbors, and family.

Chapter Nine
Being Present

Saying His Name

THERE WAS A POINT WHERE I started to notice something, and once I saw it, I couldn't unsee it.

People stopped saying his name.

It didn't happen all at once, and it wasn't something anyone announced or even seemed fully aware they were doing. It showed up in small shifts, conversations changing direction, sentences being softened, pauses where his name should have been but wasn't. It was subtle enough that you could almost question whether it was real, but consistent enough that it became impossible to ignore.

It felt like people were trying to protect me, like they believed that by not saying his name, they were sparing me from something. As if his name itself was fragile or dangerous or too heavy to say out loud without causing more harm.

And I understand that instinct, at least on the surface. Saying his name makes him real in a way that can feel uncomfortable. It brings him into the room. It asks people to acknowledge something they don't know how to fix, something they can't soften or make sense of.

But what people don't realize is that not saying his name doesn't protect me. It makes him feel like he's disappearing.

And after everything—after the loss, the grief, and the long, exhausting process of learning how to breathe again—the last thing I could handle was the idea that he was slowly being erased from the spaces he should still exist in. When people avoid his name, even with the best intentions, it creates a silence that feels like absence, and that absence carries its own kind of pain.

Because he was born so prematurely, there were people who treated his life like it didn't fully count. Like there wasn't enough time for him to have really been here, enough time for him to matter in the same way. One person even insinuated that sharing photos of him or speaking about losing him was somehow taking away his dignity, as if acknowledging him would do more harm than good.

But silence doesn't protect dignity.

Silence erases existence.

And I refuse to let that happen.

Losing him didn't just change me and his dad. It changed relationships in ways I wasn't prepared for. There are people in our lives who still don't say his name, who don't include him when they talk about grandchildren or cousins, and I feel that every single time. It doesn't have to be said out loud to be understood. It sits in the spaces where he should be, in the moments where he is left out, and it reminds me that not everyone sees him the way I do.

But then there are the moments that go the other way, the ones that stay with me for entirely different reasons.

I remember the first time someone included him without hesitation. A cousin of my husband had made something for their great grandparents and listed all of the children in the family. His name was there.

Jaxon.

Seeing his name written out, placed where it belonged, acknowledged without explanation or discomfort, meant more than I can fully put into words. In that moment, he wasn't something people avoided or stepped around. He was counted. He was remembered. He was part of us in a way that didn't need to be justified.

And that matters more than people realize. Because saying his name keeps him present. It keeps him part of the world he was supposed to exist in, even if that existence looks different now. It reminds me that he is not something that only lived in my body or in my memory, but someone who belonged here, someone who is still part of this family, whether people are comfortable with that or not.

I say his name because I need him to exist outside of just me. If I am the only one saying it, then it starts to feel like he only existed for me, and that is a weight no mother should have to carry alone. I don't need people to say it perfectly, and I don't need them to say it all the time, but I need to know that he is still seen, still acknowledged, still remembered in the spaces we share. Remembering him does not make the pain worse.

But forgetting him would.

Silence vs. Absence

Sometimes the right thing to say is nothing at all, but that doesn't mean *doing* nothing.

There is a kind of silence that can feel comforting when it's shared. It can look like sitting beside someone without trying to fill the space, allowing the quiet to exist without rushing to explain it or fix it. It can be a hand held without words, a presence that doesn't demand anything in return, or sitting with you in the weight of it. That kind of silence can feel safe.

But silence is not the same as absence, and that distinction is important. When people don't know what to say, they often don't show up at all. They avoid the phone call, skip the visit, or read the message and don't respond. It might feel like they don't care, but it's more likely that they don't know how to sit in something they can't fix. The absence becomes distance, and that distance grows quickly in a space that already feels isolating. What was already heavy becomes lonelier.

There is a difference between sitting in silence with someone and leaving them alone in it. One is shared and grounding, an acknowledgment that says, "I'm here, and you don't have to carry this by yourself." The other, even when it isn't intentional, can feel like withdrawal, like stepping back from something that became too uncomfortable to stay close to.

And for a grieving mother, that absence doesn't only feel like a lack of support. It feels like something else is being taken, too.

Because after losing a child, one of the deepest fears is that they will be forgotten. Not loudly, not all at once, but slowly, in the way people stop saying their name, stop bringing them up, and stop acknowledging that they were ever here at all. That fear sits quietly under everything, and when people stop showing up, it feeds into it in a way that is hard to explain unless you've lived it.

It starts to feel like the world is moving forward without them. And when that happens, it can feel like you're the only one left holding onto their existence. That's a weight no parent should have to carry alone.

So when you don't show up, even if you think you're giving space, it can feel like you're confirming that they didn't matter. When you don't say their name, it can feel like you're agreeing to a version of reality where they were never really here.

And that absence carries a different kind of pain.

Grieving mothers don't need you to have the right words. They don't need you to fix anything or make the pain smaller. What they need is to know that their child mattered, that they are still seen, and that their child's presence, however brief, is still acknowledged in the world around them.

That happens through showing up. It happens through saying their child's name, through being willing to sit in the discomfort without trying to rush past it, and through choosing presence even when you don't feel equipped for it. It means allowing silence to be something shared instead of something that creates distance. Because presence, even imperfect presence, will always matter more than perfectly chosen words.

What you might have meant:

"I don't know what to say."
"I don't want to make things worse."
"I don't know how to show up."

What you could have said instead:

"I don't have the words, but I'm here."
"I'm coming by. We don't have to talk."
"Tell me about them."

Say their child's name. Show up, even if all you can offer is your presence.

There was a point where the messages slowed down, where the calls stopped, and people returned to their lives while I was still sitting in mine. That shift didn't happen all at once, but when I became aware of it, it was one of the hardest parts of this experience—not the moment it happened, and not even the days immediately after, but in the quiet that came later, when the support faded and the grief didn't. That's when I realized something I didn't understand before.

Grief doesn't end when the support does.

Getting It Right

There is no easy button for grief, and there is no set of words that will make this better.

I've spent a lot of time talking about what hurts and what doesn't help, about the things people say with good intentions that still land in a way that adds weight instead of taking it away. But if I'm going to ask people to be more mindful of that, then I also need to be honest about what actually does help, and the truth is not as complicated as people think.

The first thing that has to go is the idea that there are "right words." There aren't. There is nothing you can say that will undo what happened, and there is nothing you can say that will take the pain away, especially in the beginning when everything still feels unreal and impossibly heavy. That isn't because you're doing something wrong. It's because this kind of loss doesn't respond to language in the way people want it to.

And that's where people get stuck.

They hesitate because they don't know what to say, and in that hesitation, they start to pull back. They convince themselves that if they can't say the perfect thing, maybe it's better not to say anything at all. But grief doesn't need perfect words. It needs people who are willing to show up even when they feel unprepared.

The goal isn't to stop her from feeling it. The goal is to make sure she doesn't have to feel it alone.

You cannot take away her pain, and trying to do that will only leave both of you frustrated, because there is no version of this where it suddenly becomes easier just because someone said the right thing. What you can do, though, is take some of the weight off everything surrounding her. Grief doesn't exist in isolation. It sits on top of all the normal responsibilities of life, and suddenly even the smallest tasks can feel impossible.

Making sure she has food isn't just about feeding her. It's about removing the decision-making that comes with it, the effort of planning and preparing something when even getting out of bed feels like more than she has to give. It's about making sure that when her body needs something, she doesn't have to think about how to provide it.

Taking care of the kids, even for a few hours, isn't just about giving her a break. It's about giving her space to fall apart without feeling like she is failing someone else in the process. It's about removing that impossible tension between wanting to be present for the children she still has and needing a moment to sit in the grief that doesn't go away simply because someone else needs her.

Sitting with her while she's not okay isn't passive. It's one of the most active forms of support you can offer. It means choosing to stay in a space that feels uncomfortable, without trying to rush her out of it, without trying to redirect it into something easier to witness. It means allowing her to be exactly where she is without asking her to soften it for you.

That's what helps. Not fixing it. Not explaining it. Not trying to make it smaller.

What helps is removing the things she doesn't have the capacity to carry so that she can focus on the one thing she doesn't have a choice but to carry.

And that kind of support doesn't happen once. It happens over time.

It happens when the messages stop coming from everyone else, when the world has moved on, and she is still sitting in something that hasn't changed. It happens in the follow-through, in the consistency, in the choice to keep showing up even when it's no longer new or visible or talked about as much.

Just being someone that they know they can lean on without feeling like they are "too much."

That is what it means to get it right.

The Ones Who Get It Right

There are people who get it right, and not because they have the perfect words or some special understanding of grief, but because they recognize something far more important. They understand, whether instinctively or through experience, that this isn't something they can fix, and instead of trying to shape it into something more manageable, they choose to step into it.

What sets them apart isn't what they say. It's that they show up, and they keep showing up steadily and intentionally. They are there in the beginning, when everything is loud and immediate and impossible to ignore, but what matters even more is that they don't fade when that intensity passes. When the messages slow down, when the world returns to normal for everyone else, and when the grief settles into something less visible but no less heavy, they are still there.

They don't disappear when it becomes less obvious. They don't step back when it becomes uncomfortable. They make the choice to stay, and that kind of consistency carries a weight that is hard to fully explain unless you've felt what it's like when people don't.

They don't try to give me reasons or explanations, and they don't attempt to reshape what I'm feeling into something easier to witness. There is no pressure to make it make sense, no expectation that I should be handling it in a way that feels more acceptable, and no suggestion that I should start moving forward before I'm ready. Instead, they allow me to exist exactly where I am, even when that place is heavy, even when it doesn't make sense, and even when it is difficult to sit in.

There is a kind of permission in that. Permission to not be okay. Permission to not have answers. Permission to move through it in a way that doesn't need to be explained or justified.

That kind of space is rare, and it is one of the most meaningful things you can give someone who is grieving.

Their support doesn't always look the same, but it is always rooted in the same intention. Sometimes it looks like conversation, like sitting with me and letting me talk about him without hesitation, without redirecting, and without trying to soften what I'm saying. Other times it looks like silence, not the kind that comes from avoidance, but the kind that comes from presence, where nothing needs to be said because they are already there.

It looks like food showing up without me having to think about it, without me having to ask, and without me having to feel like I owe something in return. It looks like help with the kids when I don't have the energy to hold everything together, when I need space to fall apart without feeling like I am failing someone else in the process. It looks like people stepping in quietly, removing pieces of the day that I don't have the capacity to carry, and doing it in a way that doesn't make me feel like a burden. What they give me isn't just help.

They give me room.

Room to grieve.

Room to breathe.

Room to exist in a version of myself that I don't recognize, all without asking me to rush into becoming someone else.

And what matters most is that they don't need me to be okay in order to stay. They don't wait for the version of me that has it together or for the version of me that can reassure them that things are improving. They stay with the version of me that is struggling, the version that is still trying to understand how to exist in a world that has changed.

They say his name.

They remember him.

They include him in conversations and in moments in ways that make it clear he is still part of this family, still part of this world, and still part of me. They don't treat him like something that needs to be avoided or quietly left out, and in doing that, they give me something I didn't realize I needed as deeply as I do.

They make space for him, and because they make space for him, they make space for me. That is something I carry with me, even now.

I remember who showed up.

I remember who stayed.

Not because they do something extraordinary, but because they don't leave when it would be easier to, because they choose to sit in something uncomfortable instead of stepping away from it, and because they choose presence over perfection in a way that changes everything about how this feels to carry.

They don't fix it.

But they stay, and in a time where so much feels like it is slipping away, that consistency, that presence, and that willingness to remain is something I will always be grateful for in a way that goes far beyond words.

Thoughts From Other Mothers

Linda is one of the people who gets it right.

I didn't meet her when losing Jaxon was fresh, and sometimes I think about how different those early days might have felt if I had known her then. But I know her now, and she has played an important role in helping me understand and process parts of my grief that I didn't even have words for at the time.

We didn't meet because of our losses. We met because life placed us in the same spaces, the kind of everyday moments that turn into conversations and eventually, into something more. It wasn't until later that we realized we shared this connection, and when we did, it shifted something in a way that felt both unexpected and deeply needed.

We sat on porches and talked. We shared stories that carried weight, and somehow also found space for laughter in the middle of it. She listened in a way that didn't rush anything, didn't redirect, and didn't try to make it make sense before I was ready for it to. And she laughed at my inappropriate jokes (whether she meant it or not) and that mattered more than I think either of us realized in the moment.

Because that's part of it too. Grief doesn't only need space for sadness. It needs space for everything that comes with it, including the moments that feel out of place, the humor that shows up when it shouldn't, and the pieces of yourself that are still trying to exist alongside something that changed you.

Linda gave me that space.

It wasn't forced or intentional. It was natural and steady—the kind of support that doesn't announce itself but is always there when you need it. She is what an incredible support system looks like.

The kind of support that doesn't try to lead your grief somewhere else but is willing to sit with you exactly where you are. The kind that doesn't need to have the answers because it understands that the presence is what matters most. And if I'm being honest, I wish I had known her in the beginning.

Linda B.

My experience losing my daughter was different. Every experience is. No two are the same. I was lucky to have my village—my family, around me. I had twins, and one was born sleeping. We knew ahead of time, so we weren't blindsided at delivery. My mother had a stillbirth, and my sister did as well, just a year before mine.

I heard the well-meaning comments, but I was able to take them as that: well-meaning, because honestly, the people saying them were the ones showing up with actions—and actions speak louder than words. And to be fair, my personality was already at the point where I would call a spade a spade when needed. Me talking about what happened or making things uncomfortable for others was their issue, not mine. I actually had worse comments from people (going through their own IVF grief) that said I didn't deserve to "get" twins when I announced my pregnancy.

Maybe the hardest person I had to deal with was the doctor who delivered my twins. I had an urgent c-section—not an emergency… yet. After I had delivered and was stitched back up, the doctor came to talk to me on my side of the curtain. I was still strapped to the table. My living baby had been taken to the NICU, but I was able to see her and give her a kiss (bless that baby nurse who did that for me!) before she was taken. The doctor explained the things he needed to explain, and then told me that he and the other doctor felt that I shouldn't see my daughter who was stillborn. That it would be traumatic for me.

He was trying to manage the trauma from a very difficult situation. My baby wasn't born perfect, and her look could have been hard for some.

Chapter Ten
Conclusion

For The Mothers Who May Be Reading

If you picked up this book because we are part of a club no one ever wants to be a member of, I am so deeply sorry that you're here. There are no words that make that easier, but I hope that somewhere in these pages you found something that made this feel just a little less isolating.

Maybe you're a lot like me, and there are moments when you want to shake people until they understand what this actually feels like. The gap between what you're carrying and what the world seems to see can feel impossibly wide. Maybe some of the phrases I've talked about brought you comfort when they were said to you, even if they didn't land that way for me. Or maybe there are things you've heard that aren't in this book at all, things you would add to this list because your experience looks different from mine.

That's the reality of grief like this—it doesn't follow a single path, and it doesn't fit into one explanation or one set of emotions. There is no right way to carry it, no timeline that makes sense, and no version of this where you can measure whether you're doing it "correctly."

But if there is one thing I hope this book has given you, it's the understanding that you are not alone in this, even when it feels like you are. And beyond that, I hope it gives you permission to not be okay without feeling like that is something you need to fix, hide, or move past before you're ready.

You are allowed to feel any amount of pain for as long as your heart needs to feel it. What you lost cannot be measured, minimized, or replaced. This kind of loss doesn't shrink just because time passes, and it doesn't become easier simply because the world expects it to. It exists in its own way, and learning how to live with it takes time that no one else gets to define for you.

So take that time.

Grieve in a way that feels true to you, not in a way that feels more comfortable for the people around you. If you find yourself needing to laugh, let that happen without questioning whether it's allowed. If you need to cry, let it come without trying to control it. If you need to scream, if you need to sit in silence, if you need to do nothing at all for a while, those responses are not wrong—they are part of how you move through something that was never meant to be carried in the first place.

Feeling it is not the problem.

Feeling it is part of the process.

It is how you begin to understand what it means to carry something this heavy without letting it take everything from you, even though it may feel like it already has.

At the same time, try not to lose yourself completely inside the despair. I know how easy that is, how quickly it can start to feel like no one understands and no one ever will, but that isn't the full truth. There are so many of us walking around with the same kind of broken heart, even if we don't always recognize each other in passing.

And while it may feel unfair to put anything else on your shoulders right now, you are still allowed to protect your peace in whatever way you need to. You are allowed to say when something isn't helping, to step away from conversations that feel overwhelming, and to create space when the noise of other people's words becomes too much to carry on top of everything else.

You are allowed to prioritize your own feelings in this moment without guilt or explanation.

You don't owe anyone comfort while you are still learning how to survive your own loss, and you don't have to make your grief easier for someone else to witness just so they feel less uncomfortable.

And if all you do today is make it through the day, if that is the only thing you have the energy for, then that is enough.

I Am Not Broken.

You might read this book and think, "My God… this woman is depressed."

And honestly, I get it.

This is heavy. I've laid out raw feelings—the kind most people don't say out loud, the kind that usually stay tucked behind "I'm fine" because it's easier than trying to explain what this actually feels like. So if you don't know me beyond these pages, it would be easy to assume that this is all I am.

But I want to take a moment to be clear about something that I didn't fully understand in the beginning.

I am not broken.

Now, I know that might sound contradictory. There are parts of this book where I say this loss broke me, and at the time, that's exactly what it felt like. It felt complete and absolute, like something in me had shattered in a way that would never come back together. But what I've come to understand over time is that "broken" wasn't a fact—it was a feeling. And it was a very real feeling.

It was overwhelming, consuming, and impossible to separate from who I was in those early days. But it was still a feeling, not a permanent definition of who I became. Because here's the truth.

I am not broken. I am also not perfectly fine.

I am somewhere in the middle of that, in a place that is a little messy and a little complicated and, if we're being honest, occasionally held together by caffeine, dark humor, and the decision to just keep going.

I am deeply flawed. I am sometimes inappropriate. I am not always meant for public consumption, especially before coffee or in the middle of a bad day. I have coping mechanisms that might raise an eyebrow or two, and I have absolutely laughed at things that I should not have laughed at.

But I am still here. And I am still living a life that is full in ways I didn't think would be possible when this first happened.

The grief still exists. It didn't disappear, and it didn't magically turn into something easier to carry overnight. It's still part of me, still something I feel in quiet ways that don't always show up on the outside. But I have learned how to live with it instead of feeling like I am drowning in it, and that shift is something that only came with time.

I think about Jaxon every day, and that hasn't changed. What has changed is the way it affects me. It doesn't take me down the way it did in the beginning, and that doesn't mean I love him any less or that I've moved on from him. It means I've learned how to carry him in a way that allows me to keep living at the same time.

My husband and I were married about a month after we lost him, which, depending on how you look at it, sounds either incredibly romantic or like a questionable life decision made during an emotional crisis. The truth is probably somewhere in between.

I tried really hard to push him away. I convinced myself that he didn't have to stay, that since we didn't have a child anymore, he was free to go, as if the loss of our son somehow erased the reason for him to be there in the first place. But he didn't leave. He stayed, and he loved me through all of it, through the grief, through the parts of me that were harder to love, and through the version of me that I didn't even recognize at times.

Seventeen years later, we are still here.

It hasn't been easy, and it hasn't been perfect, but it is ours. We built something in the middle of all of that, something that didn't exist before the loss but also wasn't defined by it. We built a life, a family, and something that continues to grow in ways I am grateful for every single day.

And no, I am not a total train wreck.

At least not all the time.

There are still moments that are hard, still days where it feels heavier than others, but those moments don't define my entire existence the way they once did. They are part of my life, not the entirety of it.

There were people who expected this loss to break us before we ever had a chance to begin, and there were moments where it almost did. But we didn't let it, and we didn't allow other people's expectations to determine what our life would become.

We chose each other. We chose to stay. And we chose to build something anyway. So no, I am not broken.

I am changed.

I am shaped by what I have lived through, and I carry it with me in ways that are sometimes heavy and sometimes quiet, but always real.

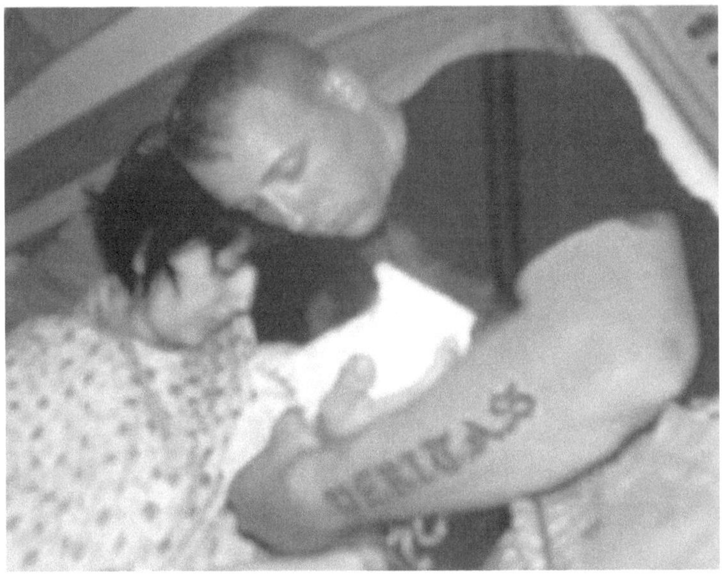

Epilogue

People who know me in real life are probably a little surprised that I've only said "fuck" a couple of times in this entire book, considering it shows up pretty regularly in my day-to-day vocabulary. So it feels appropriate to end this the way I would actually say it out loud—not polished or softened, but honest.

Sometimes, when you don't know what to say, you don't need to search for better words or try to piece together something that sounds comforting. You don't need to explain the unexplainable, and you don't need to fill the silence just because it makes you uncomfortable. Sometimes the most helpful, most respectful, and most compassionate thing you can do is nothing at all.

When you don't know what to say… just shut the fuck up.

And I don't mean that in a harsh or dismissive way. I mean it in the most real, practical way possible, because when there is nothing to say, forcing words into that space often does more harm than good. Not everything needs to be explained, and not everything needs to be softened into something easier to hear. Most of the time, what people are actually looking for in those moments isn't a sentence that makes it better—nothing can make it better. What they need is presence.

I say this to my kids' friends when they come over for birthday parties. Instead of gifts, I tell them we prefer presence over presents. What matters most isn't what you bring with you but that you showed up in the first place. And the more I've lived through this, the more I realize how much that idea applies here.

Grieving mothers don't need perfectly chosen words or carefully constructed phrases that try to make everything feel less heavy. They don't need someone to tie their loss into something meaningful or manageable so it makes more sense to the outside world. What they need is someone who is willing to show up anyway, even when it's uncomfortable, even when there is nothing to say, and even when the silence feels heavy.

Because that silence, when it's shared, doesn't feel empty. It feels like someone stayed.

You don't need to take the pain away from her, and you couldn't even if you tried. More importantly, you shouldn't want to, because that pain is not something separate from her child. It is not just grief in the way people often think of it. It is love that no longer has a place to go, love that still exists without somewhere tangible to land, and that doesn't disappear just because the person it belongs to is no longer here.

The absence that exists isn't something that should be filled. That space is there for a reason.

That space has a name. For me, that name is Jaxon.

And the pain I carry is not separate from him—it's what remains when everything else is gone. It is the shape of the love that didn't disappear when he did, the evidence that he was here, that he mattered, and that he is still part of me in a way that doesn't go away.

So when you tell a mother to move on from her pain, what you are really asking her to do is move on from her child, and that is not something she or I will ever do. It is not something most mothers will ever do, no matter how much time passes or how different their lives begin to look on the outside.

I sit with it.

I carry it.

I live with it.

And if you are someone who wants to support a grieving mother, you don't need to take that from her or try to change it into something easier to understand. You just need to be willing to sit beside her while she holds it, to stay in the space where there are no answers, and to let that be enough.

You can hold her while she holds her pain. You can remind her, without words if necessary, that she is not alone in it. And if you don't know what to say, you don't need to search for something better.

You can simply say, "I'm here."

And mean it.

Acknowledgments

LET'S BE REAL HONEST FOR A SECOND. I'm probably never going to write another book. I know "never" isn't a guarantee, but I'm going to treat this like it is, so I don't miss anything that needs to be said.

To my husband, Mark:

You and I went through more before we ever said our vows than most people do in a lifetime, and you stayed anyway, even when the world made it very clear that you didn't have to.

We didn't come out of that untouched. We fell apart together, and then, slowly, piece by piece, we rebuilt something out of what was left. What we have now isn't what we planned, but it is something real, something hard-earned, and something I wouldn't trade for anything.

So I guess what I'm saying is…

"Baby it's a fact, our love is true. The way black is black, and blue is just blue…"

(We literally walked down the aisle to Hello Goodbye, this song gets a shoutout… those are the rules.)

Thank you for never giving up on us. I love you more than there are stars in the sky.

To my children, all of you, the ones who will read this and the ones who won't:

Every single one of you is a part of my soul, and there aren't words big enough to fully explain what you mean to me. Watching you grow into the people you're becoming is one of the greatest privileges of my life, and loving you is something that exists on a level I don't think I could ever properly put into words.

And to the ones I don't get to watch grow, I miss you in a way that never goes away. You are all my reason for being, and I am so lucky to be your mother.

To my editor, Vicky:

I am both incredibly grateful and—also a little bit sorry. The guidance you gave me helped more than I can explain, even if it may have also contributed to this being longer than I originally planned. Thank you for leading me in a way that never made me feel small, never made me feel like I didn't belong here, and never made me feel like a total fuck up who had no business writing a book.

To the stand-in Grandmas, Lisa and Julie:

Lisa, you've been like a mother to Mark and me from the very beginning, stepping in when no one else was willing to fill that space. You've loved us in a way that feels steady and unconditional, and we couldn't love you more for it.

Julie, I am so sorry for how we met. I wish our beginning had been a much happier one, but I am so grateful for what grew from it. You welcomed us as family from the moment we met, and that kind of love is something I don't take lightly. It is an honor to carry on Max's name, and it's clear to me exactly where he got who he was from. He was the best because he had the best mom.

We love you so much.

To all the friends who became family, and to the ones who always have been:

There are too many of you to name, and I don't trust myself not to accidentally leave someone out, so just know that if you're reading this and wondering if I mean you—I do.

Some of you have known me for most of my life (not in a gay way. Well… kinda in a gay way), and some of you came along later and decided to stay, which honestly says a lot about your character.

From letting me romance the wrong elf without warning, to coffee chats on the front porch, to everything in between, we've built something together that goes beyond friendship. We've shared love, we've shared pain, and we've raised our kids alongside each other in a way that feels like something bigger than any one of us.

And apparently, some of you will raise them if we die… so, no pressure.

Thank you for laughing with me, and sometimes at me. For crying with me. For tolerating all of my flaws and, somehow, loving me not in spite of them, but because of them.

Most of all, thank you for showing me that family doesn't always mean blood.

We are so lucky to have the village that we do.

And lastly… and definitely least (you don't even get bold font):

To anyone who has ever bet against us or rooted for us to fail…

Suck it.

A Space For Your Story

When I put out a call for other mothers to share their stories and experiences, the response was more than I ever expected, and I don't think I was fully prepared for what it would feel like to hold that many pieces of love and loss at once.

My heart is both full and broken by the number of mothers who want—and need—their stories to be heard.

There is no way I could include them all, and that didn't sit right with me. Every story matters, every loss matters, and every child matters in a way that deserves to be acknowledged, not filtered down to what fits within the pages of a single book.

So this is your space.

If something in this book resonated with you, if you saw pieces of yourself in these pages, or if there are words you have been carrying that you've never had a place to put, I want you to use the next few pages in whatever way feels right to you.

You can write your story in full, or you can write fragments of it, the parts that feel most important or the ones that have stayed with you the longest. You can write their name because names deserve to be spoken and remembered. You can write the things people said that stayed with you, whether they helped or hurt, and you can write the things you wish had been said instead.

You can write about what carried you through, or what made it harder, or the things that no one saw but you still hold onto.

Or you can simply write how much you love them.

There is no right way to do this.

There is no structure you need to follow, no expectation you need to meet, and no version of this that has to look like anyone else's story. This space is not about doing it correctly. It is about giving your story somewhere to exist outside of your own mind and heart, even if only for a moment.

I want this book to feel like it belongs to you as much as it belongs to me, and as much as it belongs to the other mothers whose voices are held within it.

You are not alone.

And your story deserves space too.

www.ingramcontent.com/pod-product-compliance
Ingram Content Group UK Ltd.
Pitfield, Milton Keynes, MK11 3LW, UK
UKHW041955190726
13854UKWH00005B/1989

9 798995 944515